As one of the world's longest established and best-known travel brands, Thomas Cook are the experts in travel.

For more than 135 years our guidebooks have unlocked the secrets of destinations around the world, sharing with travellers a wealth of experience and a passion for travel.

Rely on Thomas Cook as your travelling companion on your next trip and benefit from our unique heritage.

Thomas Cook **traveller** guides

SOUTH AFRICA
Mike Cadman

D1352199

your travelling companion since 1873

Written by Mike Cadman, updated by Jeroen van Marle
Original photography by Mike Cadman and Trevor Samson

Published by Thomas Cook Publishing
A division of Thomas Cook Tour Operations Limited
Company registration no. 3772199 England
The Thomas Cook Business Park, Unit 9, Coningsby Road,
Peterborough PE3 8SB, United Kingdom
Email: books@thomascook.com, Tel: +44 (0) 1733 416477
www.thomascookpublishing.com

Produced by Cambridge Publishing Management Limited
Burr Elm Court, Main Street, Caldecote CB23 7NU
www.cambridgepm.co.uk

ISBN: 978-1-84848-449-8

© 2005, 2007, 2009 Thomas Cook Publishing
This fourth edition © 2011
Text © Thomas Cook Publishing
Maps © Thomas Cook Publishing/PCGraphics (UK) Limited

Series Editor: Karen Beaulah
Production/DTP: Steven Collins

Printed and bound in Spain by GraphyCems

Cover photography © Günter Gräfenhain/Huber/4Corners

All rights reserved. No part of this publication may be reproduced, stored in
a retrieval system or transmitted, in any form or by any means, electronic,
mechanical, recording or otherwise, in any part of the world, without prior
permission of the publisher. Requests for permission should be made to the
publisher at the above address.

Although every care has been taken in compiling this publication, and the
contents are believed to be correct at the time of printing, Thomas Cook Tour
Operations Limited cannot accept any responsibility for errors or omissions,
however caused, or for changes in details given in the guidebook, or for the
consequences of any reliance on the information provided. Descriptions and
assessments are based on the author's views and experiences when writing and
do not necessarily represent those of Thomas Cook Tour Operations Limited.

Contents

Background   4–29

Introduction   4
The land   6
History   10
Politics   14
Culture   18
Festivals   24

First steps   30–37

Impressions   30

Destination guide   38–139

Western Cape   38
Eastern Cape   70
Northern Cape   76
Gauteng   84
Free State   98
North West   102
Mpumalanga   104
Limpopo   114
KwaZulu-Natal   116
Lesotho and Swaziland   138

Directory   140–89

Shopping   140
Entertainment   146
Sport and leisure   152
Children   156
Food and drink   158
Accommodation   166
Practical guide   172
Language   180

Index   190–91

Maps

South Africa   7
Western Cape (incl. The Garden
   Route tour)   39
Cape Town   40
Tour: The Cape Peninsula   51
Eastern Cape   71
Northern Cape   77
Johannesburg   85
Gauteng   95
Free State and North West   99
Tour: Blyde River Canyon   111
Limpopo and Mpumalanga   115
KwaZulu-Natal incl. Lesotho
   & Swaziland   117
Durban   118
Tour: KwaZulu-Natal battlefields 132
Tour: Old Zulu Kingdom   137

Features

Wildlife   26
Some common animals of the bush 28
Townships   36
Whale watching   54
Winemaking   56
Diamonds   82
Train journeys   100
Kruger National Park   106
The 'Big Five'   108
Game reserves of Zululand
   and Maputaland   124
Eating in South Africa   164

Tours

Tour: The Cape Peninsula   50
Tour: The Garden Route   66
Tour: Blyde River Canyon   110
Tour: KwaZulu-Natal battlefields 132
Tour: Old Zulu Kingdom   136

Introduction

Table Mountain stands tall over Cape Town with its fine beaches and winelands. Almost 2,000km (1,250 miles) to the northeast, the vast expanse of Kruger National Park shelters South Africa's largest population of elephants, lions and other creatures. In between lies most of South Africa, a nation of more than 44 million people with a rich and complex social fabric, 11 official languages, a zest for sport, and a landscape that boasts remarkable geographic splendour and variety.

In KwaZulu-Natal, crystal-clear streams drain from the sometimes snow-capped uKhahlamba-Drakensberg mountains, while in the Northern Cape, cheetahs and martial eagles search for prey in the rolling grass-covered sand dunes and desert scrub of the Kgalagadi Transfrontier Park. Along the country's west coast, the icy Benguela current makes swimming a pastime only for the brave, but in contrast Africa's southernmost coral reefs are located in the warm waters along the northeast coast.

These and other geographic and climatic variations contribute to

The Durban beachfront, KwaZulu-Natal

making South Africa's flora and fauna among the most diverse of any region of comparable size anywhere.

In the middle of the country, the teeming metropolis of Johannesburg and its neighbouring towns and cities attract visitors and work-seekers from all over the country, and even from neighbouring states.

South Africa is the economic powerhouse of Africa, and although many citizens are poor, the country has an extensive and well-maintained road system, efficient air links and good tourism infrastructure. The mining industry and rich deposits of gold, diamonds, platinum and other minerals have long been the mainstay of the economy. There is, however, an increasing focus on the technology, manufacturing and tourism sectors.

In some fields the constraints of apartheid have been shed relatively quickly, and today business leaders, politicians, academics and sportsmen

African penguins, native to the southwestern coast of Africa

and -women come from all sectors of the country's diverse population. In other respects, the transition from apartheid has not been as easy, but more and more children, known locally as the 'born frees', have no memory of South Africa without democracy, a concept which arrived with the 1994 election won by Nelson Mandela and his African National Congress party.

South Africa's youth, in keeping with global trends, are part of a rapidly urbanising population, and many people live in informal settlements around cities and towns.

South Africa's cities are not old by European standards – Cape Town, the country's oldest city, was open countryside in 1652, and Johannesburg is only 125 years old – but fossil evidence reveals an ancient history of human habitation. Some of the oldest hominid fossils on record have been found near Johannesburg, and archaeologists can trace fairly constant human habitation of the region for hundreds of thousands of years.

In recent history, migrants from many parts of Africa and Europe have made the country their home, and many South Africans' lives incorporate aspects of other cultures as a matter of daily routine. Cuisine, fashion and the arts all increasingly reflect this amalgam of traditions.

The land

South Africa covers some 1.2 million sq km (463,000sq miles), which is more than twice the size of France or a bit bigger than the US states of California and Texas combined. It lies roughly between 22 and 35 degrees south of the equator, and has 2,950km (1,830 miles) of coastline washed by the Atlantic Ocean in the west and the Indian Ocean in the east.

South Africa shares borders with Namibia, Botswana, Zimbabwe, Mozambique, Swaziland and Lesotho. The latter is entirely surrounded by South Africa.

The climate varies markedly, with most of the country experiencing the greater part of its rainfall in summer. On the Highveld (literally 'the high land'), and in the uKhahlamba-Drakensberg mountains, dramatic thunderstorms sweep across the countryside on summer afternoons often disappearing over the horizon and leaving clear rain-scrubbed skies.

The Western Cape is blessed with a Mediterranean climate, experiencing warm-to-hot dry summers and cool, wet winters.

Temperatures in the interior sometimes climb to over 36°C (97°F) in summer, but in winter can plummet to well below 0°C (32°F) at night in the various mountain ranges and in the deserts. Deserts are not always hot, and although the Kalahari Desert regularly experiences daytime temperatures well over 40°C (104°F), night-time winter temperatures can drop as low as −10°C (14°F).

Most of South Africa lies on a plateau fringed by a coastal belt of varying width, and many of the basic geographic and climatic features spread across one or two, and in some cases several, provincial boundaries. The 2,300km (1,430-mile) Orange River, for example, South Africa's longest river, rises in Lesotho and then flows along the borders of the Free State and Eastern Cape. It then heads through the Northern Cape to enter the Atlantic, where the borders of South Africa and Namibia meet.

South Africa comprises nine provinces: Eastern Cape, Free State, Gauteng, KwaZulu-Natal, Limpopo, Mpumalanga, North West, Northern Cape and Western Cape.

A basic description of the geography and vegetation of each province is given below and overleaf.

South Africa

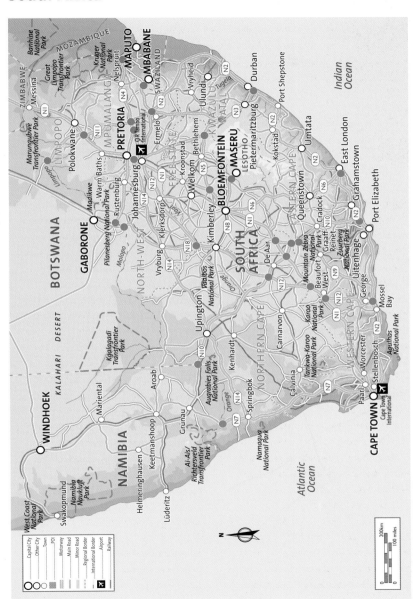

The land

Eastern Cape

Long, wide sandy beaches characterise much of the Eastern Cape coast, although in the south, high forested ridges run right down to the sea providing spectacular views from cliffs above the waves. Further north, the rugged Wild Coast, a region of sea cliffs, deep river valleys and largely empty beaches begins. Not far inland, high fold mountains that sometimes receive snowfalls roll into the low scrub semi-deserts of the Karoo (*see Eastern Cape on pp70–75*).

Free State

The Free State is primarily open grassland, which begins to dissipate into the semi-deserts of the Karoo and Kalahari in the west. In the east, high ridges with sandstone cliffs form deep valleys, and in winter heavy snowfalls sometimes occur (*see Free State on pp98–9*).

Gauteng

Gauteng is generally a region of open grassland-covered plains ribbed with low ridges and the steeper Magaliesberg to the north. Much of the province is more than 1,500m (4,900ft) above sea level (*see Gauteng on pp84–97*).

KwaZulu-Natal (KZN)

The 3,200m (10,500ft)-high uKhahlamba-Drakensberg Mountains form the western boundary of this province. South Africa's highest point,

Jeffrey's Bay, a favourite surfing spot in the Eastern Cape

Mafadi, 3,446m (11,300ft), is in the Injisuthi region of these mountains. The land falls away rapidly to the east in a jumble of rolling hills, which run down to the subtropical coast. The south coast has many rocky coves, but the beaches become sandier along the north coast (*see KwaZulu-Natal on pp116–37*).

Limpopo

Three major mountain ranges, the Waterberg, the Soutpansberg and the Northern Drakensberg, cut through this province, which is primarily open *bushveld* (grassland savannah interspersed with thorn trees). The Drakensberg form the edge of the escarpment, which drops steeply to the Lowveld (low country). The Lowveld comprises many vegetation forms, but in simple terms is dominated by *bushveld* and *mopane* woodlands, which together cover much of Kruger National Park. Summers are very hot and winters mild (*see Limpopo on pp114–15*).

The land

Mpumalanga

High-altitude open grasslands in the west, south and southeast of this province drop to the Lowveld down Northern Drakensberg passes similarly steep to those in Limpopo Province. This is an important farming province, and also includes the southern half of Kruger National Park (*see Mpumalanga on pp104–5*).

North West

Much of this province is covered by open *bushveld*, and the Waterberg Mountains act as an important watershed. In the centre of the province, the ancient Pilanesberg volcano makes a dramatic setting for the well-run Pilanesberg National Park. The west gives way to the arid Kalahari (*see North West on pp102–3*).

Northern Cape

The Northern Cape falls into the Karoo and Kalahari semi-desert zones. Much of the Karoo is covered with shrubs and sparse grasslands, and is an important cattle- and sheep-farming region. Camel thorn trees, grasses specially adapted to the dry conditions and huge skies are the trademarks of the Kalahari. In the southwest, the harsh Namaqualand region usually bursts into colour once a year as millions of flowers bloom after winter rains (*see Northern Cape on pp76–81*).

Western Cape

Although the west coast is cool and sparsely vegetated, the rest of this province's coastline is a mix of secluded coves, broad sandy beaches and mountains that plunge directly into the ocean, breakers crashing at their feet. Inland, a maze of fold mountains finally gives way to the arid plains of the Karoo, the vast region extending over four provinces. Many of the famed Cape winelands shelter on the slopes and in the valleys formed by these mountains (*see Western Cape on pp38–69*).

Hout Bay at night, Western Cape

History

100,000 BC Archaeological evidence shows southern Africa is already inhabited by *Homo sapiens*.

8000 BC San hunters inhabit parts of South Africa.

AD 1–1500 Iron-working spreads to southern Africa as Bantu people begin to move southwards and dominate the San and Khoikhoi peoples.

1488 Bartholomeu Dias rounds the Cape and reaches Mossel Bay.

1497 Vasco da Gama rounds the Cape and charts the sea route to India.

1652 Arrival of Jan van Riebeeck, first commander of the Dutch East India Company's Cape settlement.

1688 French Huguenot settlers arrive.

1779 First of nine settler–Xhosa frontier wars in the Eastern Cape.

Slave bells, Stellenbosch

1795 First British occupation of the Cape.

1806 Second British occupation of the Cape.

1820 Large group of British settlers arrive in the Grahamstown area.

Mid-1830s The Great Trek into the interior begins as Boers grow resentful of British rule in the Cape colony.

1838 Battle of Blood River: a small force of Voortrekkers defeats the Zulu.

1850s Independent Boer republics of Orange Free State and Transvaal are established.

1867 Discovery of diamonds near Kimberley – the diamond rush begins.

1879	Anglo-Zulu War: battles of Isandhlwana and Rorke's Drift.
1880	First Anglo-Boer War.
1886	Gold discovered. Johannesburg founded.
1899–1902	Second Boer War.
1910	Union of South Africa.
1912	The African National Congress (ANC) is formed.
1913	The Natives Land Act reserves most land for the use of white people.
1948	Victory for the National Party in white elections.
1950	Various apartheid measures introduced and tightened during the next few years.
1952	The ANC's defiance campaign begins.
1958	Dr Hendrik Verwoerd becomes prime minister. Apartheid strictly enforced.
1960	Referendum for South African independence. Sharpeville Massacre: demonstrators against the Pass Laws are fired on (69 killed, 180 injured). State bans the ANC.
1961	South Africa leaves the Commonwealth and becomes a republic. The ANC begins its armed struggle. ANC leader Nkosi (Chief) Albert Luthuli wins Nobel Peace Prize.
1964	Rivonia Treason Trial: Nelson Mandela and seven other ANC members are sentenced to life imprisonment. South Africa excluded from Olympic Games.

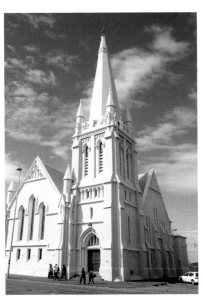

Trinity Methodist Church, East London

1966	Verwoerd assassinated.
1967	Professor Chris Barnard performs the world's first heart transplant.
1975	Invasion of Angola by South Africa.
1976	Police open fire on student protesters in Soweto on 16 June. The shootings lead to nationwide rioting, resulting in hundreds of deaths.
1977	Mandatory UN arms embargo. Steve Biko killed in police detention.
1983	A new constitution allows three separate houses in parliament – for whites, Coloureds and Indians.

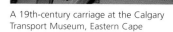

A 19th-century carriage at the Calgary Transport Museum, Eastern Cape

1984	Archbishop Desmond Tutu is awarded the Nobel Peace Prize.
1985	ANC President Oliver Tambo, Rev. Jesse Jackson and Archbishop Huddleston head a 100,000-strong march through London demanding sanctions. State of emergency declared in sections of the country. Political violence sweeps through townships.
1985–86	Thousands of people are detained without trial during continued state of emergency. Violence continues intermittently for next five years.
1989	F W de Klerk becomes president succeeding P W Botha.
1990	Nelson Mandela released from prison. The ANC and other banned political organisations are legalised. National Party government abandons apartheid, and begins negotiations to end it. The ANC suspends the armed struggle.
1992	Whites-only referendum leads to a 69 per cent vote to continue reforms.

1993	Nelson Mandela and President F W de Klerk are awarded the Nobel Peace Prize.
1994	Democratic elections in April; ANC President Nelson Mandela elected president of South Africa. South Africa re-enters the Commonwealth.
1995	The Truth and Reconciliation Commission under Archbishop Desmond Tutu is appointed to hear evidence concerning apartheid atrocities.
1999	The second democratic election is held. Mandela steps down as president. The ANC wins and Thabo Mbeki becomes president.
2004	The third democratic election is held and the ANC returns to power. Mbeki remains president.
2008	Jacob Zuma elected leader of the ANC. Riots in Gauteng townships and elsewhere leave 42 dead, hundreds injured and thousands homeless. Thabo Mbeki resigns and is succeeded as president by

HIV/AIDS

The HIV/AIDS epidemic is one of the greatest issues facing South Africa, and has enormous social and economic consequences. Many children have been orphaned after their parents have died from AIDS-related diseases. Many skilled people have been lost to the economy after falling sick.

The government was initially very slow to respond to the crisis and, in many cases, the private sector took the lead in health education and medication.

Nearly all HIV in South Africa is spread through participating in unprotected sex. Blood transfusions in large hospitals are responsible for very few cases. Private hospitals use world-class technology.

	Kgalema Motlanthe. South Africa resumes culling elephants in national parks after 14-year moratorium.
2009	The ANC wins its fourth election and Jacob Zuma becomes president.
2010	The FIFA World Cup is held in South Africa.
2011	Local elections in May see the ANC's rival, the Democratic Alliance, standing to gain considerable ground. In June, the Gautrain project is finished, resulting in Africa's fastest rail link, between Johannesburg, Pretoria and O R Tambo Airport.

Politics

South Africa in the 21st century is a country hard at work creating an economically viable, functional democracy, but at the same time is intent on enjoying the journey. The excitement and sheer relief of the first-ever democratic election in 1994, the jubilation that greeted the election of Nelson Mandela as president, and the realisation that South Africa could hold its head high in the global community of nations is old hat now. The memories of those heady days will always be treasured, however.

Now the euphoria has transformed into determination among South Africans to alleviate poverty and unemployment and to improve education and health. In recent years, the ruling party, the African National Congress (ANC), has faced criticism for its handling of these issues. Efforts have been made to provide better housing in 'informal settlements' and townships such as Soweto, but many feel that this process is taking too long, since these deprived areas continue to be a breeding ground for violent crime. Over the course of his tenure, the ANC's Thabo Mbeki, who served as president from 1999 to 2008, also encountered criticism for his handling of the economy, the ongoing AIDS crisis (he supported ineffective 'traditional medicine' over more efficacious new treatments) and his handling of South Africa's relationship with the corrupt and brutal Mugabe regime in Zimbabwe.

Yet despite the scale of the task, there is no lack of enthusiasm, and the ANC,

under the leadership of Jacob Zuma, retained power in the general election in April 2009, gaining a near two-thirds majority in what has been described as the most competitively fought election since 1994. Though it was still a convincing victory, it also showed that the ANC may face more effective political opposition in future, perhaps from a coalition between the Democratic Alliance (formed from the merger of the New National Party and the Democratic Party) and Cope (Congress of the People), a breakaway party established in 2008 by former ANC members.

Zuma himself is a controversial figure. In 2008, the same year that he displaced Mbeki as leader of the ANC after a power struggle, Zuma faced allegations of corruption and rape, of which he was acquitted. The corruption charges were dropped just before the 2009 poll. However, he has also played a role brokering peace deals in areas of political violence, and has been more outspoken than his predecessor in his criticism of Zimbabwean politics.

South Africa has had three fully democratic elections since 1994, and the latest round has shown that political debate is as vibrant as in other democracies, with voter turnout high and polling conducted peacefully. This is in stark contrast with the era of apartheid between 1948 and 1994 when a formal policy of denying black people the vote, the right to free movement and the right to employment was strictly enforced. It incorporated numerous other legalised injustices.

Discrimination against the black population in South Africa was nothing new. It dates back to 1652, when European settlers first arrived in Cape Town. Resistance manifested itself in many ways over the centuries, but only after the worsening of racial tensions when the conservative National Party (NP) came to power in 1948 did parties such as the ANC begin organised opposition in earnest.

As the political struggle intensified, widespread insurrection gathered momentum. This was met by severe state oppression, including the Sharpeville Massacre of 1960, when police shot dead 69 protesters, and the imprisonment of Nelson Mandela in 1964 after he was found guilty of treason and sabotage – thousands of people considered to be political opponents were jailed and many were tortured. The Soweto riots in 1976 were sparked after police opened fire on protesting schoolchildren, igniting nationwide unrest.

During the 1980s, the NP government clamped down hard on the popular uprising sweeping through the black townships. States of emergency were

Pretoria has been South Africa's administrative capital since 1860

declared, giving the police and military extended powers: tens of thousands of people, including children, were detained without trial. Thousands died during the conflict, many killed by police bullets. Many political books were banned – it was illegal to quote people like Mandela or even to possess his writings – and the press was censored. Political opposition was effectively outlawed by the NP.

While the state suppressed black political aspirations, white South Africans continued to enjoy very high living standards. This was at considerable cost, however, to the state's foreign relations. Throughout the closing decades of the 20th century, South Africa's political turmoil made news headlines worldwide and international sanctions against the nation (economic, sporting and cultural), coupled with travel restrictions, eventually took their toll. To exacerbate matters, the aggressive NP leadership drew South Africa deeper into expensive guerrilla wars in neighbouring states, first in Namibia and later in Angola. Consequently, by the mid-1980s, South Africa's economy was struggling and both internal and international pressure against the government was mounting.

The South African government finally relented in 1990, deciding to release Mandela and legalise political parties. Four years later, after prolonged and intense negotiations by people representing nearly all sections of South African society, Mandela ushered in a new South Africa to the salute of military helicopters flying the country's new flag and to the acclaim of a rapturous nation. South Africa's transition to democracy without a full-blown war was hailed as an example of conciliation and common sense. Since then, South Africa has maintained good relations with many countries around the globe, achieving a level of international acceptance that would have been unthinkable two decades ago.

Statue of Cecil John Rhodes in Cape Town

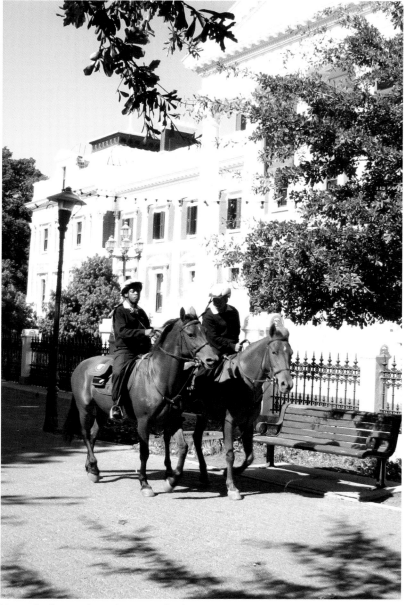

Mounted police patrol past the Houses of Parliament in Cape Town

Culture

South Africa's cultural heritage reflects the country's complex history, and African, European and Asian influences all thread their way through the art, music and literature of the region. South Africa's relatively recent transition to democracy has led to a significant shift towards exploring and embracing Africa's rich cultural background, and this heritage is actively being promoted with a greater sense of pride than at any other time in history.

Art

South Africa's oldest art form (*see box on p22*) is the rock art and engravings of the San (Bushmen). However, the 17th, 18th and 19th centuries saw the development of a school of European artists intent on creating a record of the landscapes, people and animals in what was to them a strange new country.

Perhaps the best known of these painters were Thomas Baines and Thomas Bowler, whose work created an accurate, if somewhat stylised, record of the country as it then was.

African beadwork at a fleamarket

Culture

New African art by Thabo Nyelele

Music

Whether the music is played on a cowhide drum, a *marimba* (a form of xylophone usually made from a gourd), a Stradivarius violin or an electric guitar, someone in South Africa will consider the entertainment 'traditional'. As with so many other aspects of the country, local music has its roots in many cultures and traditions, and is continually evolving according to new demands and trends. Western and African influences mix easily, and radio stations and music stores offer everything from *kwaito* (a form of rap), reggae, jazz, blues, classical and hard rock to general pop. Jazz trumpeter Hugh Masekela and singer Miriam Makeba have been known internationally since the 1960s, and younger artists such as Yvonne Chaka Chaka with her cross-cultural rhythms have built followings across Africa. The piano work of Abdullah Ibrahim (formerly Dollar Brand) has reached almost cult status in some quarters.

Johnny Clegg and his bands Juluka and Savuka pioneered a mix of traditional Zulu music and modern soft rock, and the Soweto String Quartet have managed to combine a mix of classical, jazz and African music into a huge popular product. Music is important to many South Africans, and the focal point of many a tavern or restaurant is the radio or hi-fi.

In rural areas, home-made instruments are common, and they are often ingeniously created from items

Western influence continued to dominate until well into the 20th century, but artists such as Walter Battiss slowly gave painting a more South African flavour.

Black artists including George Pemba and Gerard Sekoto, although almost unknown in South Africa at the time, took this trend to a new level in the 1940s, and today their work fetches high prices. Later in the 20th century, many artists began using their work as a form of protest against apartheid. Modern South African art draws on many influences, and increasing numbers of young South Africans are focusing on more traditional African styles. Many art galleries and markets also sell traditional African day-to-day items, including bowls, sleeping-mats and symbolic beadwork as art.

PIERNEEF MUSEUM

The J H Pierneef Museum in Graaff-Reinet displays work by landscape artist Jacob Hendrik Pierneef

designed for anything but making music. Lengths of fishing line, seeds from trees and disused motor-oil cans are adapted for use in guitars, rattles and drums.

Architecture

South African architecture is a bewildering mix of old, new, rural and modernist, with a huge dose of practicality thrown in for good measure. Older cities are a mix of glass and steel modernist structures, dull and conservative 1960s office blocks and the occasional Art Deco or Victorian building.

Sandton, part of Johannesburg, has been developed over the past 40 years, and is the largest conglomeration of new buildings in the country, with an unusual mix of avant-garde constructions, pseudo-European plazas and even buildings ostentatiously decorated with Roman-style pillars and façades.

Many of the Victorian buildings are found in Pietermaritzburg, Durban and Cape Town, but many smaller towns such as Oudtshoorn contain good examples of this style, a legacy of British colonisation. Perhaps the best-known form of South African architecture is the Cape Dutch style, prevalent from the early 18th until the mid-19th century. This is best displayed in Cape Town itself and the nearby winemaking towns of Stellenbosch, Franschhoek, Paarl and Tulbagh. Thatched-roof buildings with decorative rounded gables and white walls preside over rows of vines. Most have large, ornate double doors and square windows with carefully tended wooden frames.

The ornate Union Buildings in Pretoria – built by Sir Herbert Baker in 1912 – are, arguably, the most recognisable architectural landmarks in the country. Decorated with stone pillars and friezes, they are still used as the seat of government.

Residential architecture ranges from the opulent – built in whatever style the owner can afford – to the tiny, almost square 'matchbox' houses built as housing for black people in the formerly racially segregated townships. In poor, informal settlements, shacks are often made of corrugated-iron sheeting, wooden-crate panels and even plastic – they may not qualify as architectural masterpieces, but they are home to millions of people. In rural areas, traditional Xhosa, Zulu or Venda huts are still used, but many have been adapted over the years. Zulu 'beehive' huts were made with grass thatched over a wooden frame, although traditional Xhosa and Venda homes tended to have mud walls.

Literature

Although most South African literature is written in English or Afrikaans, the country's writers have explored a wide range of themes and social issues, and their works largely trace the development of modern South Africa. Many writers have achieved

Traditional singers on the Victoria and Alfred Waterfront, Cape Town

international recognition, and the Nobel Prize for Literature was awarded to two South Africans in recent years. Nadine Gordimer (1991) and J M Coetzee (2003). Although very different in style, both examine the psychology of apartheid and post-apartheid South Africa. The theme has been consistent among many writers, and the classics *Cry, the Beloved Country* by Alan Paton (1948), *Down Second Avenue* by Es'kia Mphahlele (1959) and *Country of my Skull* by Antjie Krog (1998) dig deeply into the country's collective psyche.

South African poetry covers a very broad range of subjects, ranging from the South African War (Anglo-Boer War), through to a celebration of nature, love and the freedom struggle. Poets, including Sipho Sepamala and Mafika Gwala, used their work to try to raise political awareness when other forms of political expression were outlawed. South Africa has also produced many writers of popular fiction – Wilbur Smith is one of the best-selling authors of all time. Although not literature in the classic sense, South Africa has a very strong publishing industry based on the environment and wildlife. A huge variety of high-quality coffee table books, field guides and popular science works is available at good bookshops.

Drama

Many South African playwrights and actors have achieved international fame. Athol Fugard and John Kani have received critical acclaim in New York, London and elsewhere.

The performing arts have a strong base and long tradition in South Africa and perhaps reached their peak in the last years of apartheid when theatre gave voice to protest that would otherwise have been silenced.

The Market Theatre complex in Johannesburg and others risked closure by running some political performances. Today, that courage has been transformed into a desire to teach, and many theatres run courses helping train aspiring actors.

Every year in June, Grahamstown in the Eastern Cape runs a week-long arts festival (*see Eastern Cape section, pp70–75*) where both established and fringe actors, playwrights and other performers strut their stuff. Various smaller festivals are hosted elsewhere in the country (*see pp24–5*).

SAN ROCK ART

Perhaps some of the most unusual art galleries in the country are the rock overhangs and shelters where San (Bushmen) artists used vegetable and animal-blood paints to record hunting, ceremonies and other scenes.

The San wandered through South Africa as long as 40,000 years ago, and left one of the largest collections of rock art in the world scattered throughout the more mountainous areas of South Africa.

Their paintings and rock engravings tell stories of their daily life, but they also had spiritual significance. The richest collections are found in the uKhahlamba-Drakensberg mountains in the Eastern Cape and KwaZulu-Natal.

African Footprint, a big, bold African musical, was a huge success and even played in China. Various symphony orchestras perform regularly, and some of the larger cities host ballets and opera, often with international guest artists performing. In poor areas, many churches and other groups run choirs which give public performances, helping to create pride and status for people who struggle to make a living.

Culture

Children dancing in Company's Gardens, Cape Town

Festivals

Most festivals in South Africa are modern events and few have the ancient traditions of those in Europe, Asia or South America. This does not detract from the fun, however, and many festivals, and some sporting events, are a good excuse for a party, something South Africans find hard to resist.

Not all festivals are held annually, and it is a good idea to check with tourism authorities about events planned in each region.

January
Cape Town New Year Carnival
Thousands of singing and dancing minstrels move through the streets of Cape Town. Everyone parties.

February
Dias Festival
Mossel Bay. Food and cultural festival.

March
Cape Town Festival
Art, music and other events.

The Cape Town International Jazz Festival

April
Rand Show
Johannesburg. A huge consumer show with everything from cars and computers to candyfloss.
Klein Karoo National Arts Festival
Oudtshoorn. Afrikaans cultural festival with theatre, music and other entertainment.
Cape Town International Jazz Festival
Two days of world-class jazz.
Port Elizabeth's Splash Festival
Watersport, music and other events.

June
National Arts Festival
Grahamstown. The biggest event of its kind in South Africa, offering theatre, music and other varied entertainment.

July
Knysna Oyster Festival
Knysna. Road-running marathons, bicycle races, oysters and other food. The town is usually packed during this popular event.

Performers at the Tshwane International Show in Pretoria

Stellenbosch Food and Wine Festival
Over 500 wines are showcased.

August
Tshwane International Show
Pretoria. The city's biggest trade fair and festival.
Winter Witblits Festival
Prince Albert. *Witblits* is powerful home-brewed alcohol, but the festival is also about food and fun.

September
Arts Alive
Johannesburg. A spring festival with theatre, music, dance and visual arts.
Hello Darling Arts Festival
Darling, Western Cape.
Hermanus Whale Festival
Hermanus. Coincides with peak whale-viewing times. Lots of events.

October
Sabie Forest Fair
Mpumalanga. A biennial festival with various forestry-related and sawmilling events, next held in 2012.

November
Cherry Festival
Ficksburg, Free State. Festival celebrating the cherry harvest.

December
Knysna Street Carnival
Holiday crowds enjoy a variety of stalls and live music.
Paternoster Crayfish and Seafood Festival
Western Cape. Lots of fresh seafood, wine and music.
Spier Summer Arts Festival
Runs until March. Concerts and other entertainment.

Wildlife

The biodiversity of southern Africa is extraordinary. Although it only comprises around 1 per cent of the earth's landmass, the region hosts more than 340 mammal species, which is about 8 per cent of the worldwide total. South Africa also hosts about 880 bird species, and more than one-quarter of all living land tortoise species. Altogether, more than 400 species of reptile occur in southern Africa – by comparison, around 300 species are found in the whole of mainland United States of America.

South Africa's biological diversity is due to the wide variety of habitats that occur in the region. They range from the *fynbos* (a variety of plants of which 67 per cent occur only in South Africa) of the western and southern Cape, to subtropical coastal forest in KwaZulu-Natal, grasslands in the central regions, and savannah in the north and northwest.

Additionally, two ocean currents flow along South Africa's coastline influencing both marine and terrestrial life. The warm subtropical Agulhas current surges down the east coast, while the cold, nutrient-rich Benguela nourishes sealife and influences weather patterns along the west coast.

Game reserves are sprinkled across the country, each with its own treasures and attractions. South Africa

Female elephants are very protective towards their young

is one of the easiest places in Africa to see the 'Big Five': elephant, lion, rhino (both black and white), leopard and buffalo.

Although these, and predators including the cheetah and wild dog, are considered to be the glamour species, many antelope and smaller species are no less interesting and deserving of attention. The very common impala, zebra, giraffe, wildebeest, baboons, warthogs and dozens of other species all fill important ecological niches and provide endless photo opportunities.

In case these creatures do not provide adequate entertainment, South Africa has many even less well-known animals. Who would not be delighted to spot a pygmy hairy-footed gerbil – a tiny 25g (1oz) rodent that lives in the western parts of South Africa – or even the short-snouted elephant shrew that lives in the hot, dry northern parts of the country?

Birds also range from the large and spectacular to the tiny and unobtrusive. The large eagles and vultures usually occur in game reserves and remote areas where food is plentiful. Lappet-faced and Cape vultures, both with wingspans of over 2.5m (8ft), and martial, bateleur and black-breasted snake eagles excite even experienced birders. Less dramatic are hundreds of other

The fastest land mammal, the cheetah, can reach a speed of 100kph (62mph)

species, including the colourful lesser double-collared sunbird and the unobtrusive fairy flycatcher, which tips the scales at just over 8g (less than a third of an ounce).

Also at the diminutive end of the scale is the world's smallest tortoise, the speckled padloper, which measures just 10cm (under 4in) across its carapace. This tortoise, which occurs only in the Western Cape, is threatened both by habitat loss and the pet trade.

Whales and dolphins are plentiful in South African waters, and in season are easily and often seen from the shore (*see Whale watching feature on pp54–5*).

In 2008, South Africa auctioned 47 tonnes of ivory (from elephants which had been legally culled) to Chinese and Japanese buyers. The sale was sanctioned by the international conservationist organisation CITES, but was widely criticised.

Some common animals of the bush

Although spotting the 'Big Five' is the highlight of a visit to the bush, there are many other animals which are no less interesting and will almost certainly be seen more often.

They all play an important role in the jigsaw puzzle of ecosystems – remove one species entirely and it affects the whole picture.

Cheetah

With its long legs and lithe body the cheetah is clearly built for speed – a design which has made it the fastest mammal on earth. Cheetahs hunt small antelope, and sometimes prey as small as rabbits, by slowly stalking them and then bursting into an explosive sprint. They tire quickly and not every hunt is successful. Cheetahs are the slightest of the large cats, with males weighing up to 60kg (132lb), and are often robbed of their kills by spotted hyenas, leopards and, sometimes, lions.

Gemsbok

Rapier-like horns are the most obvious feature of this large, powerful antelope. It lives in drier areas and happily survives in the middle of the Kalahari Desert. They do not need to drink water for most of the year, deriving all their moisture

The distinctive gemsbok

requirements from their food. Gemsbok have very sophisticated body-cooling systems and water utilisation abilities.

Giraffe

Besides their obvious size and height – males weigh up to 1,200kg (2,640lb) and stand 5m (16ft 5in) tall – giraffe, when seen up close, have wonderfully long eyelashes. Nobody is sure why

Giraffes are the world's tallest animals

this is so, but it might be to protect their eyes when browsing on thorn trees.

They are common in many of the game reserves, particularly in the northern and eastern parts of the country.

Impala

The graceful impala is one of the most common animals in Kruger National Park and many other game reserves. Many people simply drive past them because they are so common, but it's well worth spending time watching them.

Most 'lambs' are born in November, and a couple of months later can be seen gathered together in nursery groups within the herd. Only males have horns.

Kudu

The tall, handsome kudu is the most common of all the large antelope and sometimes lives quite close to farmhouses and other human habitation. The males have beautiful long, spiralled horns. Kudu usually live in small herds.

Spotted hyena

These powerful predators have had a bad press and are not in any way as cowardly as they are so often portrayed in popular stories and films. They often hunt for themselves and can bring down prey as large as a wildebeest weighing over 200kg (440lb).

Nevertheless, they are very effective scavengers too, and use their immensely powerful jaws to tear skin and crack bone that not even lions can handle.

Springbok

South Africa's national animal prefers the drier central and western regions of the country. They used to form herds hundreds of thousands strong as they followed the rains, which generate fresh grazing. Today, their population is much smaller, but springbok are common enough in game reserves and on many farms.

Steenbok

These tiny antelope are common in many parts of South Africa. Many are often seen in the same area because they form territories which they defend against other steenbok. They only weigh about 11kg (24lb).

The tiny steenbok

Impressions

South Africa is an easy country to visit. All the major centres are linked by regular flights, the road system is good, and there are excellent hotels, B&Bs, game reserves and national parks. All the major centres have a wide range of well-stocked shops, medical care is first class and the telephone system and Internet facilities are the best in Africa. The tourism industry has grown by leaps and bounds in recent years and service standards are good.

Climate

Cape Town and the southern Cape coast have a Mediterranean climate with warm-to-hot summers and mild-to-cool winters, which is when most of the rainfall occurs. Elsewhere in South Africa, most rainfall occurs in summer.

The Victoria and Alfred Waterfront, Cape Town

In many parts of the interior of the country it can become very hot in summer, particularly in Kruger National Park, Kgalagadi Transfrontier Park and parts of KwaZulu-Natal. Winter days in the interior are cool, but at night the temperature can fall below freezing. The coastal belt of KwaZulu-Natal is very humid in summer.

School holidays

Most South Africans take their annual holidays over Christmas or Easter, and more popular destinations are accordingly very busy. Although the crowds create an exciting atmosphere, tourists with some flexibility in their schedule might want to avoid these peak periods.

What to take

All the major cities are well stocked with almost any item of clothing or equipment the average traveller might need – so should anything be forgotten there is no need to panic.

Health

Good medical care and hospitals are available throughout South Africa. Consult your doctor or a travel clinic about anti-malaria medication if you intend to visit the hot northern and northeastern parts of the country, particularly Kruger National Park and the game reserves of northern KwaZulu-Natal. All tap water is drinkable. Use sunblock, even in winter, as South Africa has very high levels of ultra-violet radiation.

Access for travellers with disabilities

Although some buildings and public areas have been made user-friendly for those with mobility problems, this is not widespread. Larger airports have been designed or adapted to assist people with disabilities.

Getting around

- All the larger centres are linked by air, and cars are easily hired at airports.
- Public transport is not very good, and in smaller centres or rural areas, taxi services are poor.
- It is best to make transport arrangements at the hotel or B&B and to take advantage of local knowledge.
- Avoid the ubiquitous minibus taxis, unless you are prepared to endure bad driving and poorly maintained vehicles.
- Several reputable companies operate long-distance coaches between major centres, but be aware that distances can be intimidating. Cape Town, for example, is 1,500km (930 miles) from Johannesburg.
- There are tolls on some major roads. Cash or credit cards are accepted.
- South Africa has an extensive rail system linking most major centres. The luxurious Blue Train runs between Cape Town and Johannesburg, and is an easy way of seeing some of the countryside in comfort.

The Tsitsikamma Mountains on the Garden Route

Self-drive

It is a good idea to carry a mobile phone in case of a breakdown or some other emergency. Programme important numbers like that of the car rental company, the Automobile Association and your hotel into the phone so that you can find help easily should you experience a breakdown.

South Africans are, as a rule, poor drivers, so exercise caution on the roads. Should the driver of the minibus taxi travelling in front of you activate the hazard lights on his vehicle, it means he is about to stop, whether it is legal or not, to collect or drop off passengers. Be alert. (On major routes, drivers sometimes use their emergency flashers as a means of thanking you for allowing them to pass.)

Urban myth says that, because of the crime rate, people may feel unsafe and it is therefore acceptable to stop at red traffic lights late at night, and then continue on your way if the road is clear. It is not acceptable, and it is illegal. Wait for the green light.

Crime

This subject is always at the top of most people's list of concerns. Yes, South Africa does have an abnormally high crime rate, but the best protection against criminals is common sense. Tens of millions of South Africans use this tactic on a daily basis.

While it is important to be alert, remember the vast majority of tourists never experience crime so don't let the subject dominate your holiday.

Take sensible precautions as you would anywhere else in the world, and, if in doubt, ask your hotel, B&B or tour guide for advice.

- Don't carry unnecessary cash or valuables, and do not leave cameras or bags on the seat of your car. Store them out of sight, preferably in the boot. Lock your doors.
- It is best to take tours to some areas rather than drive yourself. Again, ask for advice. Avoid self-appointed 'guides' who approach you in the street.

Transport takes many forms in South Africa

Monkeys at Kruger National Park

• If you are ever in the unfortunate position of having someone armed with a weapon attempting to steal your car or anything else, never ever resist. The situation is unlikely to arise but, if it does, let the thieves take whatever they want.

Visiting game reserves and dealing with wildlife

Never feed wild animals, whether in game reserves or not, because the animals begin to associate humans with food. This later causes conflict with humans, and authorities end up having to shoot problem animals that are a threat. Human food also creates health problems in wild animals.

• Baboons and monkeys are particularly good at begging, extremely clever, strong, very fast and take advantage of humans in a flash. No matter how cute they look, do not feed them.

• Don't get out of the car in 'Big Five' game reserves as some species are potentially dangerous.

• If you encounter elephants while driving in a game reserve, always give them space to move off, and do not get between adults and babies. They are usually accustomed to cars and pose no threat, but it is best to give them space.

• If you have been walking through long grass, check your legs and arms for ticks afterwards. Several anti-tick sprays are available.

- Most mosquitoes start biting in the evening, so it is a good idea to wear long trousers and long sleeves if you want to avoid getting bitten. Use mosquito repellents too.

Language

South Africa has 11 official languages, and a list of useful phrases in all 11 would take up half this book.

English is widely spoken, and nearly all signage is in English. However, other languages, including Afrikaans, Zulu and Xhosa, do sometimes appear on signboards.

For the record, the 11 languages are English, Afrikaans, Ndebele, Northern Sotho (Pedi), Siswati, Southern Sotho, Tsonga, Tswana, Venda, Xhosa and Zulu.

Etiquette

South Africans are generally friendly and welcoming towards tourists. Most people are willing to offer advice and suggestions and are happy to chat with foreigners about sport, politics or whatever subject seems appropriate.

A friendly 'Hi, how are you?' will elicit an acknowledgement and probably the same question in response, which forms a good platform for any conversation.

When meeting people, a handshake is a widely accepted form of greeting. You may come across a more

complicated handshake, which involves the standard grip, and then, without releasing, slipping your hand around the other person's thumb, then returning to the traditional grasp.

Money

The South African currency is the rand (R), subdivided into 100 cents. Traveller's cheques are accepted in most banks, and credit cards are used throughout the country. ATMs are available in all major city centres and larger towns but are not so popular in smaller towns. Credit cards are not accepted for fuel. Most banks issue a separate card for fuel purchases.

Clothing

The South African lifestyle is fairly casual. In summer, many people wear shorts, casual shirts, and sandals, particularly at the coast and in game reserves. For those unused to harsh sunlight, it is wise to remember to use sunblock on legs and arms when wearing shorts and T-shirts. Dress in good restaurants is slightly more formal, but jackets and ties are unnecessary unless on business.

Before you leave

Visit the **South African Tourism** website to catch up on links to the latest shows, big sporting matches and other events that will add to the enjoyment of your trip.
South African Tourism. Tel: (011) 895 3000. www.southafrica.net

Quiet and peaceful Swellendam is one of the oldest towns in South Africa

Townships

Visitors to South Africa are often confused by the reference to 'townships' rather than suburbs or cities. Although Soweto is a huge area with a population of millions, it is usually referred to as a 'township in Johannesburg' but is in reality part of the same conurbation. The same rule applies to Kwa-Mashu near Durban, Zwide near Port Elizabeth and Mamelodi near Pretoria.

As with many things in South Africa, townships came about as a result of the apartheid policy of separate development – segregating people on the grounds of race – and

Fruit seller in Soweto

were created as residential areas exclusively for black people. Black people were only allowed into the formerly 'white' cities to provide labour, and apartheid planners decided that housing and other facilities for black people were to be kept at the most basic level possible. Most houses were tiny, almost square 'matchbox' houses with no electricity and no running water inside them. Toilets were built outside and used a night soil system where tankers collected buckets of sewage a few times a week. Initially, most roads were unpaved and street lighting was non-existent.

In terms of the policies of 'separate development', black people needed a permit to be in white urban areas, and white people needed special permission from the authorities to visit townships. Neither permit was easy to obtain and applications were often denied. Even today many white South Africans have never visited a township, despite working or playing sport with people who have lived there all their lives. Most townships were originally built with few access roads to make it easy for police to monitor comings and goings. Because the townships were intended as

Soweto is the largest township in South Africa and parts of it are still very impoverished

labour dormitories, almost no formal commercial developments such as supermarkets were allowed, forcing black people to shop 'in town' – usually the nearest city.

Today, townships are changing daily with increasing numbers of urban people having access to electricity, telephones and running water, and most roads are now tarred. Some of the informal settlements that have sprung up in and near townships still lack even these basics.

It may seem odd to treat townships as tourist attractions because, quite obviously, they are not galleries or museums. The experience is, however, well worth the time because Gugulethu is a vastly different place to the suburbs of Cape Town, as are the streets of Mamelodi and Pretoria. Every city has several townships, usually hidden out of the way, and even small towns have their own 'townships'.

They are usually lively, friendly places where everyone seems to know everyone else, a characteristic often lacking in some of the formerly 'whites-only' suburbs in many South African cities. Kids yell as they play football in the streets, and enterprising mechanics and welders repair cars by the side of the street while customers wait. Noisy *shebeens* (formerly illegal bars but still called *shebeens* even though they are now legal) are scattered along busy roads. People socialise easily and, on Sunday, many people dressed in their best outfits chat in the streets while walking to church. A tour to a township is an essential, entertaining and educational trip and should not be missed.

Western Cape

Variety is the keyword of the Western Cape. Cape Town, sheltered by the famous Table Mountain, is the gateway to this province of mountains, beaches, vineyards and a broad assortment of cultures and traditions. Both the Indian and Atlantic oceans fringe the Cape coastline. Ranges of high, craggy fold mountains roll across the province and, in the east, thick indigenous forests provide a contrast to the semi-deserts of the Karoo, which forms the northern boundary of the province.

The Western Cape's physical diversity encourages a wide variety of outdoor activity, including hiking, mountain-bike riding, kloofing (canyoning), paragliding, diving, surfing, fishing or good old sunbathing and swimming.

Although lacking the variety of big game that occurs elsewhere in South Africa, the Western Cape boasts a vast diversity of mammal, bird and reptile species with some unique attractions. The *fynbos* vegetation, which dominates the region, is the richest floral kingdom in the world hosting more than 7,300 species, 65 per cent of which occur nowhere else on the planet. The coast also offers some of the world's best sightings of

Cape Town's Victoria and Alfred Waterfront, with Table Mountain in the background

See pp66–9 for Garden Route tour

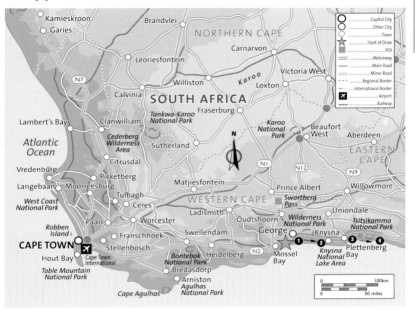

southern right whales and their newborn calves.

Closer to Cape Town, the many vineyards tempt tourists and locals alike with excellent food and wine. Throughout the region, restaurants reflect the cultural diversity of the population. Along the Cape Peninsula, small towns, including Simon's Town and Kalk Bay, have a seaside atmosphere with many good restaurants, antique shops and interesting history. Cape Town and many of the smaller centres like Darling and Hout Bay have thriving artistic communities. Theatre, music and dance performances offer a constant selection of entertainment and cultural education.

Cape Town

Cape Town is a city of beaches, mountains, good food and wine, diverse culture and a laid-back view of the world. It is also a city of great contrasts, with many poor people living in sub-standard housing, as anyone driving to the airport past the thousands of shacks on the Cape Flats cannot fail to notice. Whatever their economic circumstances, Capetonians pride themselves on knowing how to have fun and how to enjoy the scenic splendour that surrounds them. At the weekend, the beaches and mountains attract families out for picnics, and the more energetic go out riding bikes, hiking, surfing and jogging.

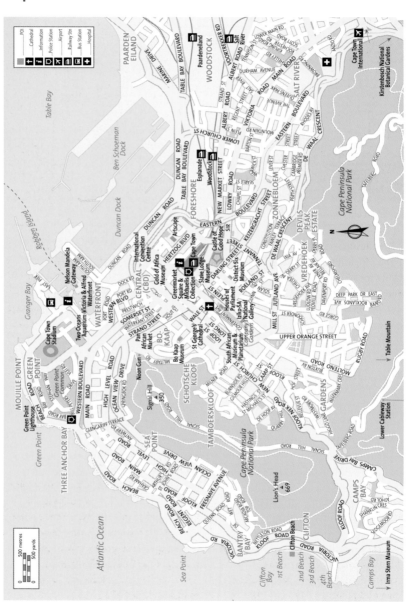

The bright old Cape Malay houses of the Bo-Kaap

Restaurants, ranging from the formal to the hip and trendy, cluster around the major beaches, the Waterfront, vineyards, and in the City Bowl itself, particularly in Kloof Street and Long Street. Cape Town is the oldest city in the country and some buildings, many of which have been restored, date back to the 17th century. Mosques, synagogues and churches attest to the many cultures that mix in the city, as do the variety of artistic styles and culinary preferences. Although many Capetonians seem to base their lives around the beaches, mountains and restaurants, the city is also home to the Houses of Parliament and several multinational corporations.

Bo-Kaap Museum

This museum is in a colourful, predominantly Muslim part of Cape Town and recreates a typical 19th-century Malay home. Many of the people who live in the area are descendants of slaves. Nearby is the Auwal Mosque, one of nine in the area. The Auwal Mosque, in Dorp Street, was built in 1798. It is recommended that visitors use one of the various companies that offer tours through this vibrant neighbourhood.

71 Wale St. Tel: (021) 481 3939.
www.iziko.org.za/bokaap.
Open: Mon–Sat 10am–5pm.
Admission charge.

Cape Flats townships

Gugulethu, Khayalitsha, Crossroads and Nyanga are home to the majority of Capetonians, and no visit to the region is complete without visiting these townships. Tour guides take in all the more politically significant areas and will happily stop at local restaurants or roadside cafés. All the townships are within sight of Table Mountain and make a startling contrast to the wealth concentrated on its slopes.

A number of township tours also take in the Bo Kaap area and the District Six Museum.
Cape Town Tourism.
Tel: (021) 487 6800.
www.tourismcapetown.co.za

Castle of Good Hope

Although the castle was built as a fort in 1666–9, it has never seen battle, and the most exciting skirmishes it has witnessed are those caused by the busy Cape Town traffic.

The outstanding William Fehr Collection of paintings, furniture and other items dating back to the arrival of the first white settlers is kept at the castle, and there is also a military museum. Tours are conducted daily (call for times), and include a visit to

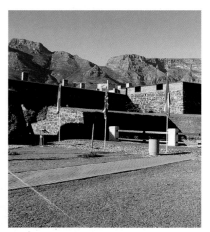

Castle of Good Hope, Cape Town

the dark and damp dungeon under the main castle. There are two restaurants in the castle grounds.
Buitenkant St. Tel: (021) 787 1260.
www.castleofgoodhope.co.za.
Open: daily 9am–4pm.
Admission charge.

Clifton Beach and Camps Bay

These are two of South Africa's trendiest and most image-conscious areas – fashion and money really matter here. The beaches are gleaming stretches of white sand that look like film sets, although the water is cold. There are no shops near Clifton Beach, but vendors sell refreshments.

By day, people visit the beaches to be seen, and in the evenings, the bars and restaurants of Camps Bay are packed. In summer, it is light until quite late in Cape Town (about 9pm), and Camps Bay is a good place to watch the sun set.

Company's Gardens

The paths through these gardens meander past some of Cape Town's best-known buildings, including the Houses of Parliament, St George's Cathedral, the South African National Gallery and the South African Museum. Many people merely use the gardens as a way of escaping some of the bustle of the city, and on sunny days dozens of office workers and others sit on the lawns under the large old trees.

The Dutch East India Company established the gardens in 1652 to grow vegetables to supply their staff and

Company's Gardens is a peaceful haven in the middle of the city

25A Buitenkant St.
Tel: (021) 466 7200.
www.districtsix.co.za. Open: Mon
9am–2pm, Tue–Sat 9am–4pm.
Closed: Sun. Admission charge.

Gold of Africa Museum

This museum contains a large and unusual collection of gold masks, animals and other artwork from all over Africa, but primarily West Africa. Goldsmiths from Ghana and Mali are particularly skilled and many examples of their work are on display.

Artefacts from Zimbabwe and elsewhere are also featured in the museum. The building which houses the museum was built in 1783.
Martin Melck House, 96 Strand St.
Tel: (021) 405 1540.
www.goldofafrica.com.
Open: Mon–Sat 9.30am–5pm.
Closed: Sun. Admission charge.

Greenmarket Square

This is a good place for some casual shopping while strolling through the centre of the city. At the fleamarket, based in the cobbled square, stallholders sell a huge variety of curios, clothing and odds and ends. There are lots more formal shops in the area as well as a number of restaurants.
Corner Burg St and Longmarket St.

Groot Constantia

This is one of Cape Town's most elegant buildings, and is the oldest wine estate

passing ships. The gardens are open all day, but be cautious of 'street kids' who sometimes snatch bags or jewellery (see box on p45).
Upper Adderley St.

District Six Museum

A good example of apartheid's brutal policy of racial segregation is presented in the pictures, maps, newspaper articles and displays in this museum. District Six was a thriving community of mixed-race South Africans, until the government of the day decided they should be moved out of sight of central Cape Town, and bulldozed the entire neighbourhood.

Some of the workers at the museum used to live in the area, and each has a sad story to tell of how their homes were destroyed. People are slowly moving back into District Six, and tours can be arranged.

Hout Bay backs on to Table Mountain National Park and the Twelve Apostles

in the country. Established by Cape Governor, Simon van der Stel, in 1685, the estate has a reputation for fine red wines, but the white wines are pretty good too. Napoleon Bonaparte's time in exile on Saint Helena island in the South Atlantic was made a little easier by supplies of wine from this estate!

The **Manor House Cultural Museum** is well worth a visit too. There are two restaurants and, on good days, you can order a picnic and sit in the tranquil gardens to admire the wonderful views.
Groot Constantia Rd.
Tel: (021) 795 5140.
www.iziko.org.za/grootcon.
Open: daily 10am–5pm.
Admission charge to museum.

Houses of Parliament
During debates, parliament can be etty noisy with vigorous heckling, but you never know when you may spot a tired MP snoozing! Tour guides help explain the workings of the South African political system and the history of the buildings, which were built in 1884 and opened in 1885.
Parliament St.
Tel: (021) 403 2266.
www.parliament.gov.za.
Open: Mon–Fri. Tours on the hour from 9am–noon. Booking required.
Free admission.

Hout Bay
Although many regard Hout Bay as being a separate town from Cape Town, it is part of the greater city. The Chapman's Peak Drive offers phenomenal views across Hout Bay. Further along, as the road winds along the mountainside, there are also great views of the wide expanse of Noordhoek Beach. There is a variety

of hotels and bars, including those on the Mariner's Wharf, which are good places for sundowners.

A toll is charged for vehicles using Chapman's Peak Drive.

Irma Stern Museum

Some of Irma Stern's best expressionist works are displayed here, as well as her personal collection of international art. Stern (1904–96) lived in the house for nearly 40 years, and her studio has been kept as it was when she worked there. The museum sometimes hosts exhibitions of other artists too.

Cecil Rd, Rosebank.
Tel: (021) 685 5686.
www.irmastern.co.za.
Open: Tue–Sat 10am–5pm.
Admission charge.

Iziko-SA National Gallery

Some art-lovers spend a whole morning or longer at this gallery, which

Kirstenbosch National Botanical Garden

is considered by many to be one of the best in the country. There are comprehensive displays of South African and international art from different periods, including paintings, beadwork, sculptures, ceramics and textiles. Some exhibitions are changed regularly, but others are permanent.

Government Ave, Company's Gardens.
Tel: (021) 467 4660.
www.iziko.org.za/sang.
Open: Tue–Sun 10am–5pm.
Admission charge.

Kirstenbosch National Botanical Gardens

A seemingly endless variety of flowers, succulents, trees and shrubs adorn the carefully tended gardens and manicured lawns that sweep up towards the steep, forested mountain slopes above. Kirstenbosch's splendid setting is alone worth the visit, but these gardens, founded in 1913, are famous among botanists worldwide

---

STREET KIDS

'Street kids' are homeless youngsters who live on the streets of South Africa's larger cities. Many abuse drugs, and in particular sniff glue. Sadly, some of these children resort to crime as a means of surviving. They usually work in groups with one child distracting the victim as the others snatch bags, necklaces or any other item they can grab. Many also beg at traffic lights.

It is best to resist giving them money, because it is often used to buy glue. There are several organisations and shelters that try to offer these children better lives.

for the variety of indigenous plants grown here.

There are also many rare plants of scientific and educational interest. Through careful selection, there are displays of flowers throughout the year, and in summer, concerts are held in the gardens. A variety of walks ranging from short ambles to a 6km (3³/4-mile) trail have been laid out in the 560-hectare (1,380-acre) gardens. A restaurant serves light meals and there is also a shop.
Tel: (021) 799 8783. www.sanbi.org.
Open: Apr–Aug 8am–6pm,
Sept–Mar 8am–7pm.
Admission charge.

Long Street

Antique shops, bookshops, music stores and any number of bars and restaurants line this street, which has a rather Bohemian atmosphere. The clubs may be somewhat smoky and noisy and might not be to everyone's taste, but Long Street provides an indispensable view into Cape Town's young multicultural set.

Michaelis Collection

Works by Rembrandt, Frans Hals, Jan van Goyen and other 16th- and 17th-century Dutch and Flemish artists such as Anthony van Dyck and Teniers form the core of this museum. Most were donated by the British-born businessman Sir Max Michaelis in 1914, and are displayed in the Old Town House. This was built in 1755 in

A restaurant on trendy Long Street

Cape Rococo style, and was once used as the town hall.
Greenmarket Square. Tel: (021) 481 3933. www.iziko.org.za/michaelis.
Open: Mon–Fri 10am–5pm, Sat 10am–4pm. Entrance by donation.

Pan African Market

Set over three floors, more than 30 stallholders sell a variety of African arts from all over the continent. The market is billed as 'Africa under a roof'. People from countries as far away as Mali, Nigeria, Cameroon and Ethiopia sell their work here, and other migrants gather at the Kalukuta Republik Book Café to chat, have a meal or listen to poetry readings. This is an excellent place to get exposure to different African cultures.
76 Long St.
Tel: (021) 426 4478.
www.panafrican.co.za.
Open: Apr–Aug Mon–Fri 9am–5pm, Sat 9am–3pm; Sept–Mar Mon–Fri 8.30am–5.30pm, Sat 8.30am–3.30pm.

Ratanga Junction

Cape Town's amusement park has over 23 rides, catering both to small children and thrill-seeking adults. Highlights are the Cape Cobra, a suspended looping roller coaster that catapults riders along an 800m (2,625ft) track at up to four times the force of gravity, the Crocodile Gorge boat ride, the children's Diamond Devil 'runaway mine train' roller coaster and the Slingshot 'skycoaster'.
Century City Boulevard. Tel: (021) 550 8744. www.ratanga.co.za. Open: School holidays 10am–5pm.

Robben Island

'The Island', just off Cape Town, holds an almost mythical aura for many South Africans as a place of banishment and incarceration. It was here that Nelson Mandela was held for most of his 27-year imprisonment. His cell and those of other leaders are visited by thousands of people, many doing so in a form of pilgrimage to these icons.

The quarry on Robben Island where Nelson Mandela was forced to work

The prison has been turned into a museum explaining the role of the leaders of the liberation struggle and the brutal history of the island, which, from the 17th century, was used as a penal colony.

Much of the seashore surrounding the island is a nature reserve, and African penguins are common.
Tel: (021) 413 4220 (museum), (021) 412 4233 (tours). www.robben-island.org.za. Tours: Ferries leave the Nelson Mandela Gateway at Victoria and Alfred Waterfront four times daily at 9am, 11am, 1pm & 3pm. Book well in advance. (All departures dependent on the weather.) Admission charge.

Signal Hill and Lion's Head

These two landmarks provide fantastic views of central Cape Town, the Waterfront, the beaches at Camps Bay, Clifton and also Robben Island. They also help emphasise the sheer scale of Table Mountain soaring over the city.

Every day, the **Noon Gun**, an old cannon, is fired from Signal Hill with an explosion that is audible all over Cape Town. The tradition dates back to 1822 when the Noon Gun was used to allow ships in harbour to set their clocks accurately.

Once you have checked your watch, the nearby restaurant is a good place for a bite to eat or a drink.
Military Rd, Signal Hill. Tel: (021) 787 1257. Open: Mon–Sat. Free admission.

Slave Lodge Museum

Part of South Africa's darker history is that of slavery in the Cape. The Slave Lodge Museum building was first used to house slaves brought to the Cape. In subsequent years, it was used as a brothel, a post office, a jail, a library and later housed the Supreme Court. Now a museum, there are displays detailing Cape Town's history and, surprisingly, even material from ancient Greece and the Far East.

49 Adderley St. Tel: (021) 460 8242. www.iziko.org.za/slavelodge. Open: Mon–Sat 10am–5pm. Admission charge.

South African Museum and Planetarium

South Africa's oldest museum has many exhibitions displaying cultural history, wildlife, rock art and fossils. In the

Table Mountain cableway

TABLE MOUNTAIN NATIONAL PARK

Nearly every mountain between Table Mountain and Cape Point, a distance of some 60km (37 miles), falls into this park (formerly Cape Peninsula National Park). The park is the richest botanical area for its size on earth, and a variety of mammals, birds and fish are also protected. It is an unusual national park in that it falls entirely within a metropolitan area. There are hundreds of kilometres of hiking trails along the mountains and beaches, although there is limited accommodation within the park and at Cape Point. Most people merely stay in urban areas and walk straight on to beaches or the mountainsides.

Tel: (021) 701 8692. www.tmnp.co.za

neighbouring planetarium, the southern skies can be explored. The museum is large and takes a while to explore.

Some of the more unusual displays are the Linton Panel containing San rock art and the Lydenburg Heads, some of the earliest African sculptures. In the Whale Well, there is, among other displays, a complete 20m (65ft)-long skeleton of a blue whale.

25 Queen Victoria St. Tel: (021) 481 3900. www.iziko.org.za/planetarium. Open: daily 10am–5pm. Closed: Christmas Day & Good Friday. Admission charge.

Table Mountain and cableway

'The view', wrote botanist William Burchell in 1822 after being inspired to climb Table Mountain, 'is singularly grand.' It remains so now. For just under four centuries the 1,087m

(3,566ft)-high mountain has been the focal point of Cape Town, influencing weather patterns and even people's attitudes. It forms a bold northern front of a high range stretching 60km (37 miles) to Cape Point. The mountain's slopes and ravines offer dozens of walks and climbs from the easy to the severe, while the cable car transports passengers to the summit's viewing platforms and restaurants.

Lower Cableway Station, Tafelberg Rd. Tel: (021) 424 0015 (office), (021) 424 8181 (weather line). www.tablemountain.net. Opening hours vary according to season. Also check weather conditions as the cable station may close in bad weather.

Two Oceans Aquarium

Spending time at the Two Oceans is a bit like taking a fantastic scuba-diving trip without getting wet. Shoals of deep-sea fish, sharks, rays, coral reef displays, turtles, seals and penguins all provide hours of education and entertainment. For those who are prepared to get wet, there are interactive displays where children can touch some sea creatures, and qualified divers can even arrange for visitors to swim in the tank where the sharks live.

The aquarium is home to fish and marine life from both South Africa's warm east coast and cold west coast waters.

Dock Rd, V&A Waterfront. Tel: (021) 418 3823. www.aquarium.co.za.

The Victoria and Alfred Waterfront is at the centre of Cape Town's working harbour

Open: daily 9.30am–6pm. Feeding times, daily: 11.30am & 2.30pm (penguins); 3pm (predators); 11am & 2pm (seals). Admission charge.

Victoria and Alfred Waterfront (V&A Waterfront)

Once disused harbour land, the Waterfront is a vast collection of hugely popular shops, curio stores, restaurants, cinemas and museums. Many of the restaurants overlook the water, and in good weather the walkways and piers fill up with people enjoying a drink or a meal, while watching activity in the working harbour.

Several hotels are part of the complex. Ferries leave from here for Robben Island and sunset cruises along the coast.

Open: daily.

Tour: The Cape Peninsula

The Cape Peninsula's mountain chain curves south from Cape Town, dips at Constantia Nek, rises at Constantiaberg, falls away over Silvermine to the Fish Hoek Valley, then swings past Simon's Town to the southeast. For 12km (7½ miles) it blends into the unspoiled wilderness of the Cape of Good Hope Nature Reserve (now part of the Table Mountain National Park), before finally tumbling into the sea at Cape Point.

Allow one day. In the centre of Cape Town, take Somerset Road at its junction with Buitengracht Street and continue along Main Road through Sea Point to the M6.

Simon's Town on the Cape Peninsula

1 The Atlantic seaboard

Sea Point's Promenade is a favourite stretch for slow walks or faster jogs. Nearby is the magnificent new Cape Town Stadium. Further on, at Bantry Bay, little Saunders Rock Beach with its tidal pool offers safe bathing.

Beyond, Clifton has the country's most fashionable beaches. Next door, Camps Bay's beaches are sprawled dramatically at the foot of the magnificent Twelve Apostles. The road winds on past Bakoven to Llandudno, picturesquely climbing up steep slopes, with Sandy Bay, a nudist beach, beyond.
The M6 climbs the hill above Llandudno, then descends towards Hout Bay.

2 Hout Bay

Wood (*hout*) was obtained here for early Cape Town buildings. The town has a lovely beach, waterfront development and a fishing harbour, which is the centre of the snoek industry and base of the crayfishing

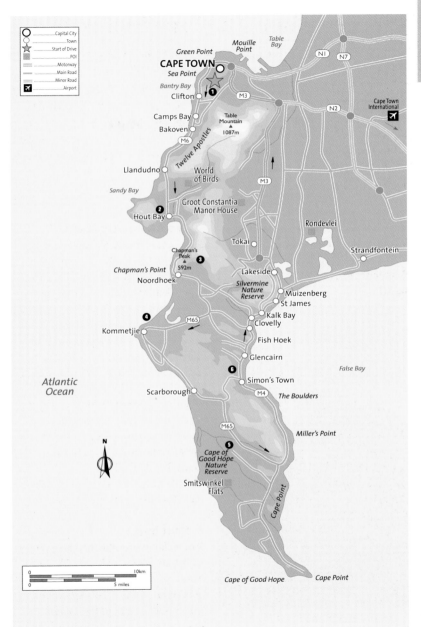

Capital City
Town
Start of Drive
POI
Motorway
Main Road
Minor Road
Airport

Table Bay

Mouille Point

Green Point
CAPE TOWN
Sea Point

N1
N7

Cape Town International

Bantry Bay
Clifton
❶
M3

N2

Camps Bay
Bakoven
Table Mountain
▲ 1087m

Twelve Apostles

Llandudno
World of Birds

Sandy Bay

Groot Constantia Manor House

Hout Bay ❷

Rondevlei

Strandfontein

Tokai

Chapman's Peak ❸
▲ 592m
Chapman's Point
Noordhoek

Lakeside

Silvermine Nature Reserve
Muizenberg
St James

Kommetjie ❹
M65
Kalk Bay
Clovelly

Fish Hoek

Glencairn
❻

False Bay

Simon's Town

Scarborough

The Boulders

Atlantic Ocean

M4

Miller's Point

M65

Cape of Good Hope Nature Reserve ❺

Smitswinkel Flats

Cape Point

N

Cape of Good Hope
Cape Point

0   10km
0   5 miles

fleet. The **World of Birds** bird sanctuary is in the Hout Bay Valley.
Return to the M6, and follow the signs to Chapman's Peak.

3 Chapman's Peak

The 10km (6-mile) drive around Chapman's Peak to Noordhoek is one of the world's most spectacular scenic passes, with exceptional views across the bay. It gives access to excellent climbs and mountain walks.
From Noordhoek, follow the M6. After the first traffic lights, the M65 branches right to Kommetjie.

4 Noordhoek and Kommetjie

Noordhoek's lovely 6km (3³/₄-mile) Long Beach is favoured by horseback

The dramatic False Bay coast

riders. At its end, Kommetjie is a quiet village with a popular surfing beach. A shallow tidal pool provides safe bathing for children.
From Kommetjie, the M65 continues through Scarborough to the Cape of Good Hope.

5 Cape of Good Hope Nature Reserve

This magnificent 7,750-hectare (19,150-acre) nature reserve is included in the Table Mountain National Park. It straddles the peninsula's tip and is home to mountain zebra, bontebok, eland and baboons.

There are drives and places to picnic and swim. The view from Cape Point across False Bay, so-called because it was often mistaken for Table Bay, is spectacular.
Tel: (021) 780 9204.
www.sanparks.org.
Open: daily. Admission charge.

At the exit, turn right if you want to visit the southern tip, then return north, turning right on to the M4 to Simon's Town.

6 False Bay

The approach to Simon's Town is via The Boulders, where the swimming, among huge boulders, is shared with a colony of African penguins. Simon's Town, South Africa's largest naval base, is a quaint seaside town, beyond which is Fish Hoek – a popular resort with wide, safe beaches.

Hout Bay from Chapman's Peak

Kalk Bay, with antique, junk and craft shops, is home to the False Bay fishing fleet. Beyond, St James has a small beach with a tidal pool. Alongside it, Muizenberg's magnificent beach offers safe bathing. Visit the **Simon's Town Museum** and **Rhodes Cottage**.

Simon's Town Museum.
Court Rd. Tel: (021) 786 3046.
www.simonstown.com/museum.

Open: Mon–Fri 10am–4pm, Sat 10am–1pm. Closed: Sun.
Admission charge.
Rhodes Cottage. Main Rd, Muizenberg.
Tel: (021) 788 1816.
Open: daily 10am–4pm. Donation.

Continue on the M4 past Lakeside, and follow the signs to the M3 and the city.

Whale watching

The southern Cape is one of the best places in the world for land-based whale watching. Every year, between June and November, large numbers of southern right whales are spotted all along the coastline.

The whales migrate from the cold southern oceans to the warmer coastal waters to mate and give birth, before beginning the long journey south to their primary feeding grounds again. They are often seen close to shore with their calves, which measure about 5m (16^1/$_2$ft) at birth.

Humpback whales are also often spotted, although in smaller numbers and usually further north along the KwaZulu-Natal coast as they migrate to their calving and mating grounds near Madagascar. Both species of whale tend to gather in small groups.

Whale watching on the southern Cape

The largest number of southern right whales usually congregate between False Bay and Hermanus, where the sea cliffs make ideal viewing platforms from which to watch them.

The whales sometimes 'breach', lifting most of their bodies out of the water, before crashing in again with a huge splash. They also 'sail' with their heads underwater and their tail flukes protruding into the air. Humpbacks display more regularly and in even more spectacular fashion. It is believed that these displays are part of courtship and other social rituals.

Both species of whale were hunted heavily in the past. The southern right whale is so-called because it floats when killed, and was considered the 'right' whale to hunt, but since hunting restrictions were imposed, their numbers have begun increasing fairly quickly.

The whale-watching industry has boomed in recent years, particularly around Hermanus, and several companies specialise in both land- and boat-based whale watching. The boats are strictly regulated, and it is illegal to approach the whales too closely.

There are a wide variety of B&Bs and hotels in the southern cape, as well as good restaurants. The area is busy in whale-watching season, which usually reaches its peak in September and October.

Many other species of whale occur in South African waters, as do 12 species of dolphin. Common, bottlenose, dusky and humpbacked dolphins are often seen along the coast. Near Sodwana Bay on the KwaZulu-Natal coast, swimmers often mingle with dolphins near shallow reefs.

Southern right whales

The southern right whale grows to a maximum length of 15–17m (49–55ft) and weighs 50–65 tonnes (49–64 tons). They are not deep divers and seldom stay submerged for more than 20 minutes. They eat small crustaceans (krill) found relatively close to the surface. Little is known of their social structure, but the mothers form very strong bonds with their calves.

Humpback whales

These whales grow to about 14m (45ft) in length and feed on small crustaceans (krill) and small fish. They weigh between 25–40 tonnes ($24^1/_2$–39 tons).

Humpback whales are well known for their 'songs' – a series of squeaks, moans and whistles of varying pitch – which can last up to 30 minutes. They usually stay submerged for a fairly short time, seldom longer than 15 minutes.

Winemaking

The South African wine industry has grown by leaps and bounds in recent years and has developed a considerable export market. There are hundreds of small boutique vineyards scattered throughout the Western Cape, cheekily rubbing shoulders with the big well-established vineyards.

Franschhoek, Stellenbosch and Paarl are the best-known South African wine-producing regions, but clever winemakers in towns like Worcester, Robertson and Montagu, some 180km (110 miles) from Cape Town, have now leapt into the market. Wealthy business people and foreigners who vie with each other to hire the best and most innovative winemakers have bought numerous vineyards.

Winemaking and fruit-growing provide economic sustenance for entire valleys in the Western Cape. Even people not directly involved in the cellars earn their livelihoods from associated businesses like restaurants, craft shops, cheese-making and tourism.

Many vineyards offer wine-tasting tours and others run good restaurants on their properties too. Each region – in all, there are 17 recognised wine routes – offers organised tours, although many tourists opt to drive themselves and spend a few days in the scenic winelands.

Whitewashed, gabled houses, surrounded by vines, sheltering in valleys beneath high fold mountains, make for picturesque touring conditions ideal for enjoying good wine and food.

All the regions offer other activities, including horse riding and hiking, and trout, yellowfish and bass fishing. There are a wide range of B&Bs, guest farms and lodges throughout the winelands.

Although experts consider South African red wines to be superior to

Grapevines thrive in the Western Cape region

the whites, many new winemaking techniques and cultivars have been developed to make the most of local conditions. Cabernet Sauvignon, Shiraz and Merlot are the most common reds, although the local Pinotage cultivars are also popular. There is a large range of whites with Chardonnay, Chenin Blanc and Sauvignon Blanc being the choice of many cellars.

South Africa's winemaking history dates back some 350 years, and the first vineyards were planted in 1655. Some vineyards can trace their origins back to the arrival of the French Huguenots in the 17th century.

South Africa also makes excellent sherry and fortified wines (better known as port, although European Union trade regulations forbid the use of the more familiar name). Brandy is also produced in some areas, and there is even a brandy-tasting route.

It is well worth buying one of the many wine guides on offer. One of the best is John Platter's *Guide to the Wines of South Africa*.

The Darling wine route is less than an hour's drive from Cape Town

The Swartberg Pass runs between Oudtshoorn and Prince Albert

Cape Town environs

There are dozens of beautiful places within easy reach of Cape Town. The best known are the winelands which stretch inland from the city boundaries through Stellenbosch, Franschhoek and Paarl and then along the east coast to Walker Bay. There are good beaches all along the coast between Cape Town and the Garden Route, and mountain ranges cut through the entire region. Many pretty villages and towns are also within easy reach of Cape Town.

Bontebok National Park

The beautiful bontebok antelope has prospered in this national park, which is South Africa's smallest. The antelope was hunted to the verge of extinction, and this park has played an important role in the recovery of the bontebok, which only occurs in the Western Cape. Cape mountain zebras and a variety of smaller antelope, birds and reptiles also occur here. The reserve protects an important area of shrub *fynbos*, which has been ploughed up for wheat fields elsewhere in the region.

The park is close to Swellendam. *Bookings: SA National Parks Central Reservations. Tel: (012) 428 9111. www.sanparks.org*

Cape Agulhas/Arniston

Cape Agulhas is Africa's most southerly tip, despite the commonly held belief that it is Cape Point. Nearby, the thatched-roofed and white-walled houses of Arniston have been declared national monuments, and white, windswept beaches have a harsh beauty.

Cape Agulhas is about 100km (60 miles) south of Swellendam. On the way, the Shipwreck Museum at Bredasdorp has a display of artefacts collected from the many ships wrecked along this coast.

The nearby De Hoop Nature Reserve offers protection to a wide array of vegetation, mammals and sealife. The marine reserve along the shoreline extends 5km (3 miles) out to sea.

Whales are often spotted here, usually from August to October.
Witsand Tourism.
Tel: (028) 537 1010.
www.witsand.com

Cederberg Wilderness Area
The 162,000-hectare (400,296-acre) wilderness area covers the rugged peaks and valleys, which provide good hiking and a huge variety of plant life. The towns of Citrusdal and Clanwilliam make good bases from which to explore the mountains and surrounding farms. After good rains, many flowers cover the *veld*, although they are not usually as prolific as those

further north in Namaqualand (*see pp79–80*). The area is about 220km (138 miles) north of Cape Town.
Cape Nature Conservation.
Tel: (021) 426 0723 for hiking permits.
www.capenature.org.za
Citrusdal Tourism Bureau.
Tel: (022) 921 3210. www.citrusdal.info
Clanwilliam Tourism Bureau.
Tel: (027) 482 2024.
www.clanwilliam.info

Ceres
This town can only be reached by one of three scenic mountain passes, and is one of South Africa's premier deciduous fruit-growing areas.

A country shop and café near Ceres

Ceres is named after the Roman goddess of fruitfulness, and has a good climate with more than 230 days of sunshine a year on average.

Various tours of fruit farms can be undertaken, as well as visits to nearby game reserves and San rock art sites; there is also hiking, mountain biking and fishing. The town is about an hour and 40 minutes' drive from Cape Town.

Ceres Tourism. Tel: (023) 316 1287. www.ceres.org.za

Franschhoek
The beautiful Franschhoek Valley is one of South Africa's premier wine-producing areas, and has become an extremely fashionable place to live and to holiday.

In 1688, the Cape Governor, Simon van der Stel, granted French Huguenot

The Franschhoek Valley is home to over 40 wine estates

Kite-surfing in Langebaan

village of Langebaan is a useful stopover when visiting the park, which is around 100km (60 miles) north of Cape Town.

Some 46km (29 miles) north of Langebaan is the small fishing village of Paternoster, which is well known for its crayfish and other seafood. Many people come here for weekend lunches and to photograph the whitewashed fishermen's houses.

The nearby Columbine Nature Reserve protects a variety of coastal plants and wetland birds.
Langebaan Tourism Bureau.
Tel: (022) 772 1515.
www.langebaaninfo.co.za

refugees land in the valley, which earned the area its name meaning 'French Corner'.

Today, most estates in the valley offer wine tasting, and many have excellent restaurants. The region caters specifically for tourists, and there are numerous art and curio shops as well as delicatessens offering local products. There are many scenic drives through the valley, and it is also worth visiting the Huguenot Museum.
Franschhoek Wine Valley and Tourist Association.
Tel: (021) 876 3603.
www.franschhoek.org.za

Langebaan
The Langebaan Lagoon forms part of the West Coast National Park, and is an internationally important birding wetland. Whales are sometimes spotted from the shore, and in August and September there are usually good showings of wild flowers. The nearby

Ostrich eggs in Oudtshoorn (*see p62*)

Stellenbosch is packed with distinctive Cape Dutch-style houses and churches

Oudtshoorn and the Cango Caves

Oudtshoorn used to be the ostrich feather capital of the world, and

The Paarl vineyards produce some of the world's best red wines

exported tonnes of these once-popular fashion items to Europe in the late 19th and early 20th centuries. Even now, ostriches are widely farmed, but these days meat and leather are more important products than feathers, and many farms also put on ostrich shows and races. Tourists can also ride on the ungainly creatures, the largest of the world's birds.

Many Victorian and older buildings line the streets of the town. The chambers and stalactites and stalagmites of the **Cango Caves** lure tourists underground some 32km (20 miles) north of Oudtshoorn. An hour-long guided tour takes visitors through the large main caves, but the system runs much deeper under the Swartberg mountains.

Cango Caves. Tel: (044) 272 7410.
www.cango-caves.co.za. Open: daily
9am–4pm. Admission charge and
guided tours.
Oudtshoorn Tourism Bureau.
Tel: (044) 279 2532.
www.oudtshoorninfo.com

Paarl

Paarl (The Pearl) is another important winegrowing centre and, although it may not share the intrinsic charm of Stellenbosch or Franschhoek, the wines are no less delicious.

Although the town was established in the early 18th century, the area had been settled and farmed since the late 1600s. Despite the focus on wine farming, other agriculture is also important. There are also pleasant walks in the nearby Paarl Mountain Nature Reserve.
Paarl Tourism Bureau.
Tel: (021) 872 4842.
www.paarlonline.com

Stellenbosch

Stellenbosch is perhaps the town most often associated with South African wine, and was founded by Dutch Governor Simon van der Stel in 1679. The town, its culture and its economy revolve around the wine industry and the University of Stellenbosch.

The Drostdy Museum in Swellendam (*see p64*) was built by the Dutch East India Company

There are many fine examples of Cape Dutch architecture, with some of the best examples in Dorp, Church and Drostdy streets. There is a variety of museums for those tired of tasting wine and eating good food in the surrounding vineyards.

Stellenbosch Tourism Bureau.
Tel: (021) 883 3584.
www.stellenboschtourism.co.za

Swellendam

South Africa's third-oldest town is built on the slopes of the Langeberg mountains and close to the wide Breede River – scenery that complements the whitewashed walls of the town's many old buildings.

The town was established in 1743 and, soon after, in 1746, the building which now houses the **Drostdy Museum** was constructed. The museum incorporates several other nearby buildings with displays of period furniture, clothing and art. The

CAPE MOUNTAIN PASSES

Dozens of steep mountain passes with magnificent scenery are a feature of the Western Cape and the Garden Route. A whole range of skilfully designed roads cut from the coast through the fold mountains to the interior. Further inland, the passes are no less spectacular, and many are worth travelling through merely for the scenery. Some of the better known are the Swartberg Pass near Prince Albert, the Du Toits Kloof Pass (use the old main road) between Paarl and Worcester, the Prince Alfred Pass near Knysna, the Franschhoek Pass and the Outeniqua Pass near George.

Dutch Reformed Church, although only built in 1911, includes Baroque, Gothic and eastern architecture.

The nearby Marloth Nature Reserve has a network of hiking trails through the mountains.

Drostdy Museum.
Tel: (028) 514 1138.
Open: Mon–Fri 9am–4.45pm,
Sat & Sun 10am–3.45pm.
Swellendam Tourism Bureau.
Tel: (028) 514 2770.
www.swellendamtourism.co.za

Tulbagh

Church Street in Tulbagh has no fewer than 32 national monuments – all classical Cape Dutch buildings, with whitewashed walls and thatched roofs, dating back as far as 1754. Most of the cottages were severely damaged or destroyed in a rare earthquake in 1969, but were all lovingly restored to their former glory.

The Oude Kerk Volksmuseum contains displays telling the story of the earthquake and the restoration project. The De Oude Drostdy Museum, which was built in 1804, is a fine example of Cape Dutch architecture.

The area also has many wine estates, restaurants and B&Bs. The more energetic can go horse riding or cycling through the pretty valley, or undertake hikes of varying levels of strenuousness.

Tulbagh Tourism Bureau.
Tel: (023) 230 1348.
www.tulbaghtourism.org.za

Tulbagh is packed with pretty Cape Dutch houses

Tour: The Garden Route

The Garden Route is one of South Africa's most scenic drives. Skirting the Indian Ocean, and occasionally dipping inland through lush nature reserves, forest, high mountain passes and lakes, this is a coast of holiday towns and resorts. The Knysna and Tsitsikamma regions are covered in dense indigenous forest, and in places steep cliffs drop directly into the sea. Accommodation is plentiful, and activities range from hiking to watersports and golf. The region is very busy at Christmas and Easter.

See map p39 for route.

Allow at least three days.
Start in George.

1 George and the Wilderness National Park

George is one of the biggest towns on the Garden Route (*www.tourismcape gardenroute.co.za*), and flying into its airport is a convenient way to start a tour of this wonderful area. The internationally renowned Erinvale Golf Course is on the outskirts of town. Founded in 1811, George has various museums and buildings of interest, including the **Outeniqua Railway Museum**.

The Wilderness National Park just east of George protects a series of coastal lakes that form an important refuge for water birds. The road that hugs the cliffs near Wilderness offers stunning views of the beaches and the coastal railway line (being repaired after storm damage at the time of writing).

Outeniqua Railway Museum.
Tel: (044) 382 1361.
www.outeniquachootjoe.co.za.
Museum open: May–Aug Mon–Fri 8am–4pm, Sat 8am–2pm; Sept–Apr Mon–Sat 8am–5pm.
Call to confirm times as the schedule sometimes changes.

Continue along the N2 for 62km (38 miles) to Knysna.

2 Knysna and the Swartberg Pass

Built around a huge, scenic lagoon, Knysna (pronounced 'nice-nah') has grown into one of South Africa's most popular tourist resorts. Open to the sea between high sandstone cliffs called The Heads, the lagoon is an important nursery for fish and other sea life, and is also used for a wide variety of watersports. In the middle of the lagoon, Thesen Island, which used to be home to a timber processing plant, is worth a visit as its industrial

Knysna's waterfront is lined with restaurants and shops

Knysna Heads

buildings have recently been transformed into stylish restaurants, shops, hotels and homes. There are many good beaches near Knysna, including Noetzie, 10km (6 miles) to the south, which has a luxurious lodge built in the form of a castle and broad secluded beaches surrounded by forest.

Plettenberg Bay

The best beaches are located around 10–15km (6–10 miles) west of the town. Nearby, the exceptionally scenic Swartberg Pass begins its climb through South Africa's largest patch of indigenous high forest – some 36,000 hectares (89,000 acres) containing yellowwood and stinkwood trees. *Knysna Tourism. Tel: (044) 382 5510. http://visitknysna.co.za.*

Continue along the N2 to Plettenberg Bay.

3 Plettenberg Bay and Robberg Peninsula

'Plett' is one of South Africa's most fashionable beach resorts. The long, broad, gently curved beach attracts many sun-worshippers at Christmas, but out of season it is quiet. The Robberg Peninsula, which is part of the Robberg Nature and Marine Reserve, juts out into the sea south of the town and offers pleasant walks and broad vistas. Nearby, Keurbooms River also has good beaches and a river estuary. *Continue along the N2 to the Tsitsikamma National Park.*

4 Tsitsikamma National Park

Running for about 80km (50 miles) along the coast, and 5km (3 miles) out to sea, the park is a spectacular ribbon of forest deeply incised by rivers that have cut their way through the mountains to the sea. The indigenous forest still has some examples of huge yellowwood trees, and a variety of hiking trails meander through the forest and *fynbos.*

The five-day Otter Trail takes in the area in all its splendour, as the path follows the coast along high cliffs and through the forest and river crossings.

Otter Trail bookings can be made through South African National Parks Central Reservations, and need to be made as far as a year in advance. *Tel: (012) 428 9111. www.sanparks.org*

Suspension bridge over the mouth of Storms River in Tsitsikamma National Park

Eastern Cape

Eastern Cape locals are often quietly smug that 'their' broad beaches, numerous mountain ranges and historical sites are seldom deluged with the crowds that Cape Town or Durban sometimes receive. The residents and tourism authorities here are only too happy to welcome tourists, but they are quick to point out that their province is a good place to 'get away from it all'. The climate is mild and ideal for holidays all year round.

Port Elizabeth

Although a fairly sedate provincial city, Port Elizabeth is well placed to make the most of good but quiet beaches and interesting history-rich countryside. The city also makes a convenient base from which to visit the Addo Elephant National Park and the scenic Baviaanskloof Wilderness Area.
Nelson Mandela Bay Tourism.
Tel: (041) 582 2575. www.ibhayi.com

Bayworld Complex

Dolphins, fossils and reptiles are all features of this complex, which unsurprisingly incorporates a museum, dolphinarium and snake park.

The museum exhibits a wide range of natural and cultural history displays, and the dolphinarium presents daily shows. Nearby, the snake park has an impressive range of residents.
Humewood. Tel: (041) 584 0650. www.bayworld.co.za. Open: Mon–Sun 9am–4.30pm. Call to confirm times of dolphin shows. Admission charge.

The Nelson Mandela Metropolitan Art Museum (formerly King George VI Art Museum and Gallery)

The museum houses various exhibitions from the Eastern Cape and elsewhere in South Africa, as well as international art, including Chinese

Grahamstown's cathedral dominates the skyline

textiles and Indian miniature figurines.
1 Park Dr, Port Elizabeth.
Tel: (041) 506 2000.
www.artmuseum.co.za. Open: Mon,
Wed–Fri 9am–6pm, Tue, Sat & Sun
1–5pm. Free admission.

No 7 Castle Hill Museum

This museum is housed in one of the
oldest settler cottages in Port Elizabeth.
The cottage was built in 1827 and has
been restored to its original state.
Various displays reflect the lifestyle of
the 1820 settlers.
7 Castle Hill, Central. Tel: (041) 582
2515. Open: Mon–Fri 10am–4.30pm.
Admission charge.

Grahamstown

Today, Grahamstown is a small
university town, but in the early 18th
century, it was a turbulent frontier post
where European settlers clashed regularly
with the Xhosa over land and cattle.

The cathedral is the focal point of the
town, which has many old buildings
that have been restored to their
original condition.

For ten days at the end of June and
beginning of July, the town hosts South
Africa's largest arts and theatre festival,
which attracts thousands of visitors.
Grahamstown Tourism.
63 High St. Tel: (046) 622 3241.
www.grahamstown.co.za

Elephants in Addo National Park

History Museum
Part of the Albany Museum, this building houses three art galleries and three cultural history galleries.
Somerset St. Tel: (046) 603 1100.
www.ru.ac.za. Open: Mon–Fri 9am–1pm & 2–5pm, Sat 9am–1pm.
Admission charge.

National Arts Festival
Tel: (046) 603 1103. Call to confirm dates and bookings.
www.nafest.co.za

South African Institute for Aquatic Biodiversity
One of several museums in Grahamstown explaining social and natural history, the Institute for Aquatic Biodiversity is the most unusual, and contains one of the most comprehensive collections of aquatic life anywhere in the world.

Somerset Ave. Tel: (046) 603 5800.
www.saiab.ac.za.
Open: Mon–Fri 8am–5pm.
Admission charge.

Addo Elephant National Park
Originally created in 1931 to protect the last 11 elephants found in the region, this reserve now has a healthy population of over 450 elephants. This is the largest elephant population south of those in Kruger National Park and KwaZulu-Natal. The thick vegetation also supports black rhino, antelope and other smaller creatures.
Addo is about 70km (45 miles) northwest of Port Elizabeth.
National Parks Board Central Reservations. Tel: (012) 428 9111.
www.sanparks.org.
Open all year.

East London, Port Alfred and King William's Town
Wide, open beaches and pleasant farming land make this region popular as a family holiday destination. There are good swimming beaches, hiking trails and nature reserves.

Amathole Museum
This museum is home to a collection of exhibits of 19th-century local life, Xhosa culture and a large display of South African mammals. Huberta, a hippo who walked more than 1,000km (620 miles) down the South African coast in the late 1920s and early 1930s,

is preserved here. (Nobody knows why she walked that far.)
Albert St, King William's Town.
Tel: (043) 642 4506.
www.museum.za.net.
Open: Mon–Fri 9am–4.30pm, Sat 9am–1pm. Closed: Sun. Admission charge.

Ann Bryant Art Gallery

This gallery exhibits work by contemporary Eastern Cape artists, along with a collection of earlier South African art.
9 St Marks Rd, East London.
Tel: (043) 722 4044.
www.annbryant.co.za.
Open: Mon–Fri 9.30am–5pm, Sat & public holidays 9.30am–12pm. Closed: Christmas Day & New Year's Day.

Calgary Transport Museum

Houses a collection of restored vehicles, including horse-drawn carts and gypsy caravans.
13km (8 miles) north of East London on the N6 to Stutterheim.
Tel: (043) 730 7244. Open: daily 9am–4pm. Closed: Good Friday & Christmas Day. Admission charge.

East London Museum

This museum contains the world's only dodo egg and also has a preserved specimen of a coelacanth, a fish thought to have gone extinct some 80 million years ago, rediscovered in 1938.
Entrance in Dawson St.
Tel: (043) 743 0686.
Open: Mon–Thur 9.30am–4.30pm, Fri 9.30am–4pm, Sat 10am–1pm, Sun 10am–3pm. Closed: Christmas Day & Good Friday. Small admission charge.

Gately House

This was the residence of the first mayor of East London and was declared a national monument in 1973. It is furnished in period style and contains original furniture.
1 Park Gates Rd. Tel: (043) 722 2141.
Open: Tue–Fri 10am–1pm & 2–5pm, Sat & Sun 3–5pm. Closed: Mon. Admission by donation.

Wild Coast

This remote coastline of sea cliffs, broad lagoons and open countryside

East London's town hall

Eastern Cape

runs from just north of East London all the way to KwaZulu-Natal. A variety of hotels and smaller lodges are dotted all the way along the coast, which is still relatively undeveloped and would suit people looking for a quiet beach holiday away from the main tourism beat.
Wild Coast Tourism.
Tel: (047) 531 5290.
www.wildcoast.co.za

Amatola Mountains and Hogsback

These mountains, some 200km (125 miles) north of Port Elizabeth and 120km (75 miles) northwest of East London, are one of South Africa's better-kept secrets. Many parts of the range are grasslands, and there are extensive forests which are ideal for hiking, climbing, mountain biking and fly-fishing.

The village of Hogsback is quaintly reminiscent of England, and makes a good base to explore the region. There are no fewer than 23 waterfalls in the area.
Eastern Cape Tourism Board.
Tel: (043) 701 9600.

Mountain Zebra National Park

This park was originally established to save the Cape mountain zebra from extinction. It has succeeded in that goal to the point that some animals have been relocated to repopulate other Karoo parks.

Nature trails and walks cross the 6,536-hectare (16,150-acre) reserve, and the diverse wildlife includes kudu, springbok and birds.
Booking through SA National Parks Central Reservations.
Tel: (012) 428 9111. www.sanparks.org.
Open: all year round.

A B&B and its lush grounds, Hogsback

Graaff-Reinet

Many of Graaff-Reinet's historic flat-roofed Karoo cottages, Cape Dutch and Victorian buildings have been colourfully restored. The town makes an eye-catching contrast to the semi-desert scrub that covers the mountains around the town.

More than 200 buildings in the town have been declared national monuments, including the **Old Library Museum**, which houses a large collection of fossils (*corner Church St and Somerset St; tel: (049) 892 3801. Open: Mon–Fri 8am–1pm & 2–5pm, Sat 9am–3pm, Sun 9am–4pm. Admission charge*). The town was founded in 1786.
Graaff-Reinet Publicity Association. Tel: (049) 892 4248.
www.graaffreinet.co.za

J H Pierneef Museum

This restored Cape Dutch house (*see picture p20*) contains landscape paintings by Jacob Hendrik Pierneef.
Tel: (049) 892 6107.
Open: Mon–Fri 8am–5pm, Sat & Sun 9am–noon. Admission charge.

Reinet House

Formerly the Dutch Reformed Church parsonage, this is an exquisite example of Cape Dutch architecture, and is now a museum with displays explaining the region's history.
Tel: (049) 892 3801. Opening times as for Old Library Museum, above. www. graaffreinet.co.za. Admission charge.

The Owl House, Nieu-Bethesda

Close to Graaff-Reinet

About 55km (34 miles) north of Graaff-Reinet (close in Karoo terms) is Nieu-Bethesda village where the **Owl House** (*www.owlhouse.co.za*) is a monument to the reclusive sculptor Helen Martins (1898–1976). Hundreds of her sculptures fill the garden, while the house is a dream world of murals, mirrors and eerie lighting.

Camdeboo National Park

Some 16km (10 miles) outside Graaff-Reinet, the Valley of Desolation offers fantastic views across the plains and mountain ranges of the Karoo. The region is rich in fossils, a legacy of the period more than 300 million years ago when marshes and moist forests covered the landscape.
Tel: (049) 892 3453. Reserve office: Bourke St, Graaff-Reinet.
www.graaffreinet.co.za

Northern Cape

The Northern Cape is South Africa's most sparsely populated province, and shares remote borders with Namibia and Botswana. The province is primarily a sheep and cattle farming region, although Kimberley, the largest city, owes its existence to the rich deposits of diamonds first found there over 130 years ago. Near Kimberley are the important South African War battle sites of Modder River and Magersfontein. The huge Kgalagadi Transfrontier Park to the north is a premier tourist destination.

Kimberley

In July 1871, the first diamonds were discovered at Colesberg Kopje (a *kopje* is a small hill), around which Kimberley, initially a tent-town of fortune seekers, sprang up.

The entire hill was dug away as miners found more and more diamonds. In later years, even more miners continued digging straight down until they had created Kimberley's famous 'Big Hole', which is 800m (2,625ft) deep. More than 14 million carats of diamonds were extracted.

Today, it is part of an open museum, which incorporates entire streets of turn-of-the-century buildings. The Boers besieged the city during the South African War, but many of the old buildings have been preserved. There are several other good museums and art galleries in the city. One of these is the Sol Plaatjie House, with galleries of displays detailing the lives of black people during the war and in later years. Plaatjie was one of the founders of the ANC. The William Humphreys Art Gallery and Duggan-Cronin Gallery contain important South African and international art works. The McGregor Museum details the cultural and natural history of the region.

The 'Big Hole', Kimberley, was one of the richest sources of diamonds ever found

Duggan-Cronin Gallery
Egerton Rd. Tel: (053) 839 2743.
Open: Mon–Fri 9am–5pm.

Kimberley Mine Museum and 'Big Hole'

Tucker St. Tel: (053) 833 1557.
Open: daily 8am–5pm. Closed:
Christmas Day & Good Friday.
Admission charge.

Kimberley Publicity Association

Tel: (053) 832 7298.
www.kimberley.co.za

McGregor Museum

1 Atlas St. Tel: (053) 839 2700.

Open: Mon–Fri 9am–5pm.
Admission charge.

Sol Plaatjie House

32 Angel St. Tel: (082) 804 3266.
Viewing by appointment Mon–Fri
8am–4pm. Admission charge.

Wildebeest Kuil Rock Art Centre

Barclay West Rd. Tel: (053) 833 7069.
Open: Mon–Fri 9am–4pm, Sat, Sun &
public holidays 10am–4pm.
Admission charge.

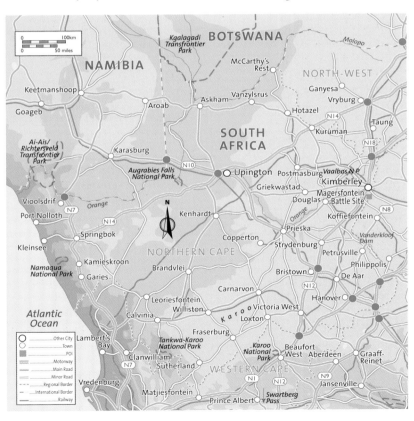

The Augrabies Falls on the Orange River

William Humphreys Art Gallery
Cullinan Crescent. Tel: (053) 831 1724.
www.whag.co.za. Open: Mon–Fri
8am–4.45pm, Sat 10am–4.45pm, Sun
2–4.45pm. Admission charge.

Near Kimberley
The battles of Magersfontein and
Modder River were fought in 1899
during the South African War and its
campaign to relieve Kimberley.
Magersfontein was one of the worst
British defeats of the war, but there
were many clashes in the area, not least
the Siege of Kimberley, which lasted
124 days.

There is a small museum at the
Magersfontein battle site.
The Magersfontein battle site is 30km
(19 miles) from Kimberley on the airport
road to Modder River. Tel: (053) 833
7115. Open: daily 8am–4.30pm.
Closed: Christmas Day & Good Friday.

Augrabies Falls National Park
Although they are far off the beaten
track, these falls are worth visiting
if travelling to the Kgalagadi
Transfrontier Park. The broad Orange
River dominates life in the arid
Northern Cape and is the focal point
of the 18,000-hectare (44,500-acre)

Augrabies Falls National Park. Here, the river is channelled into an 18km (11-mile) ravine, which becomes a maelstrom of thundering white water and spray as it crashes over ledges 56m (184ft) and 35m (115ft) high. The falls are among the largest in the world. The park protects many desert and semi-desert plant species as well as antelope, including the gemsbok and springbok.

SA National Parks Central Reservations. Tel: (012) 428 9111. www.sanparks.org

The Kgalagadi Transfrontier National Park covers red sand dunes and dry river beds

Kgalagadi Transfrontier National Park

This vast expanse of Kalahari Desert supports a surprising amount of wildlife, including lions, gemsbok, springbok, wildebeest, eland and many smaller animals. It is one of the best places in South Africa to see cheetah.

Although classified as a desert, much of the Kalahari consists of open, grass-covered plains interspersed with thorn trees and lightly vegetated sand dunes. The former Kalahari Gemsbok National Park (SA) and the Gemsbok National Park (Botswana) have been amalgamated into the Kgalagadi Transfrontier Park, which is some 3.8 million hectares (9¹/₂ million acres) in size.

The park is 260km (160 miles) north of Upington, and distances in the park, are large, so careful thought is required when planning a visit. Many companies also offer tours to the park.

SA National Parks Central Reservations
Tel: (012) 428 9111. www.sanparks.org

Namaqualand

A vast area of the Northern Cape's huge semi-desert is a Cinderella environment. Most of the year, it is harsh and dry, but after the winter

---

TRANSFRONTIER PARKS

Several transfrontier parks have been created between South Africa and its neighbours. Many of the more remote regions have declared wildlife areas on both sides of the international border. Authorities have agreed that, where possible, fences should be taken down to allow the free flow of wildlife, and tourists, across the borders. This helps create larger and more diverse wildlife areas under the joint management of the nations involved.

These include the Kgalagadi Transfrontier Park (South Africa and Botswana) and the Great Limpopo Transfrontier Park (South Africa, Zimbabwe and Mozambique). Several other transfrontier parks are being developed.

The dramatic Swartberg Pass

rainfall (mid-August to mid-September) it is transformed by millions of brightly coloured daisies, mesembryanthemums, aloes and other flowers. The towns of Springbok, Garies and Hondeklipbaai (Hondeklip Bay) are usually the best starting points from which to see the flowers, but it is worth checking with authorities first to find out where rain has fallen.

Springbok is also a good point from which to visit the remote Richtersveld National Park, which is botanically unusual with many rare species. The mountain desert scenery is arid, rocky and cut by jagged ravines. It is home to the semi-nomadic Nama people who

have recently won back the right to graze their animals and run some tourist concessions in the park.

De Beers run tours and 4×4 trips to their rich diamond-mining concessions. These concessions are found along restricted areas of the remote windswept western coastline, which has a large population of Cape fur seals.

De Beers Diamond Coast tours. Kleinsee. Tel: (027) 807 0028. www.coastofdiamonds.co.za

Central Karoo

The Karoo, in its various forms, extends from the Western Cape deep into the

Northern Cape, Free State and Eastern Cape.

Approximately 150–300 million years ago, various deposits were laid down in the vast swamps and soggy jungles that covered the area. Today, the region is rich in fossils, both of animals and plants.

Although it is an arid zone, the Karoo supports a wide range of wildlife and farming activity.

The clear and, in winter, cold skies of the Karoo make it a great place for serious astronomers and casual star watchers alike, and South Africa's largest telescope is located at Sutherland.

Karoo National Park

High mountains and wide open plains are part of the attraction of this 32,000-hectare (79,000-acre) park, which protects a wide range of animals and birdlife. Hundreds of years ago, tens of thousands of springbok migrated across these plains but, these days, numbers are far smaller, due to the guns of countless hunters.

The park preserves a good cross-section of typical Karoo habitat and supports springbok, kudu, buffalo and smaller game. No fewer than 20 pairs of black eagles nest in the park.

An award-winning rest camp with Cape Dutch-style cottages and restaurant has been developed.

The nearby town of Beaufort West is the largest in the region and the centre of a large sheep-farming community.

SA National Parks Central Reservations.
Tel: (012) 428 9111.
www.sanparks.org

Matjiesfontein

This 19th-century resort is popular with weekenders from Cape Town. The restored Victorian Lord Milner Hotel and some other buildings in the tiny village are national monuments. The hotel was used as a hospital during the South African War. The luxury Blue Train stops here on its journey between Cape Town and Johannesburg. The town is 260km (162 miles) northeast of Cape Town.

Prince Albert and the Swartberg Pass

Sheltering at the foot of the Swartberg Pass is the pretty village of Prince Albert, which is a welcome change from the dusty plains of the Karoo.

The steep pass climbs through the Swartberg mountains, and the view across the range and the plains below are spectacular.

Prince Albert farmers take advantage of the plentiful water run-off from the mountains to grow grapes and olives, and the village has several good restaurants. There are lovely walks and hikes in the mountains and around the village, and the rural atmosphere makes a fine getaway destination.

Prince Albert Tourism Bureau.
Tel: (023) 541 1366.
www.patourism.co.za

Diamonds

The discovery of diamonds marked a turning point in southern Africa's development from a rural, forgotten corner, dominated by the British Empire, to a repository of riches that in time would touch the lives of nearly everyone in the region. Diamonds are still a source of South Africa's wealth.

The first diamond discovered was the Eureka (1867), near Hopetown in the Northern Cape. Further finds occurred in 1869 on the farms Bultfontein and Dorstfontein. In 1871, fabulously rich finds were made at Colesberg Kopje, which eventually led to the development of Kimberley.

Life was probably hell for the fortune-seekers who had flocked to the site, although some of them did indeed make fortunes – and not just as prospectors.

Cut and uncut diamonds

Diamond boats, used to collect alluvial diamonds

Entrepreneurs started coaching companies, or provided such necessities as bars. The biggest headache of all was establishing ownership of this diamond-rich territory. It was called Griqualand West by the respective governments of the Free State and the South African Republic, and by the Cape Colony. It had been claimed by the Griqua, who had lived there for 70 years. In the end the British simply annexed it to the Cape (1880).

Kimberley was the cradle of the hugely profitable diamond industry that grew up in southern Africa. No one could ever have dreamt of the riches that the 'Big Hole' would yield. As digging continued, and the hole got deeper, squabbles broke out as miners struggled to get to their prize at ever more perilous depths.

This led to the amalgamation of smaller workings, heralding the era of the big mining companies. About 20 years after the first diamond had been discovered, the De Beers mine, controlled by Cecil John Rhodes, owned virtually the entire diamond industry. Since Rhodes, and under the Oppenheimer dynasty of Ernest, Harry and now Nicky, De Beers has become one of the world's largest and most profitable mining companies.

Gauteng

Almost 120 years ago, the world's richest gold deposits were discovered near what is today Johannesburg. Prospectors, speculators and the merely hopeful flocked from across the globe to the sweeping grasslands and ridges of the South African Highveld in search of success and fortune. Today, the modern office towers and efficient infrastructure of Johannesburg, its glitzy sister city Sandton and nearby Pretoria act as similar symbols of hope, offering jobs and opportunity to people from all over southern Africa.

Gauteng is the economic heartland of South Africa and, although it is the country's smallest province, at just 16,548sq km (6,389sq miles), it generates more than a third of the nation's gross domestic product (GDP).

The region is home to some of the most powerful mining companies in the world, and boasts the largest concentration of technology, financial services and manufacturing expertise in Africa.

Gauteng has a long history of human habitation, and archaeologists have unearthed some of the world's oldest hominid fossils dating back some 3.3 million years at several sites – most notably at the Sterkfontein Caves, 45 minutes north of central Johannesburg. The name Gauteng is Sesotho for 'Place of Gold', probably from the Dutch *goud* (gold).

The climate is comfortable, with warm summers and cool, clear winters, although the region's high altitude – it is on average about 1,600m (5,250ft) above sea level – sometimes results in icy nights.

Johannesburg

Johannesburg and its satellite city Sandton are the symbols of the upwardly mobile in South Africa. A widespread perception is that here everything happens faster, and that everything is bigger and better than elsewhere. This belief is reflected in the expensive cars, big houses, fashionable shops and upmarket restaurants. But the region is also one of many contrasts. Whereas the stores in Sandton carry famous clothing labels and jewellery brands, shops in the nearby dormitory areas of Soweto and Alexandra stock only basic foods and other household essentials.

A tour to Soweto or Alexandra provides an important insight into the development of South Africa, and also offers a glimpse of energetic, largely cheerful township life.

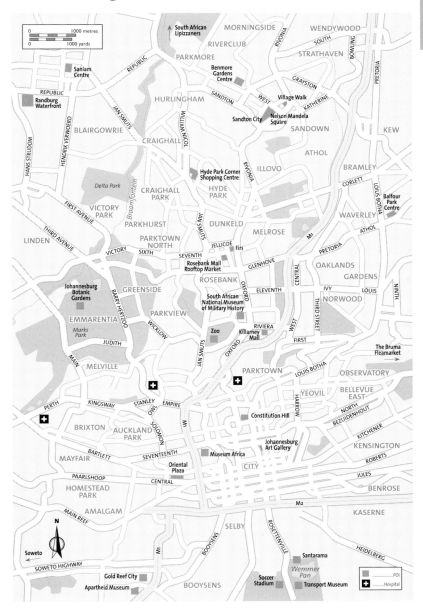

Johannesburg

Downtown Johannesburg bustles with traders and shoppers from throughout the region. Colourful fabrics decorate storefronts, and informal chefs roast *mealies* (corn) on street corners.

An evening spent at the Market Theatre or a club in the Newtown Precinct will confirm the cultural diversity of the city, as will a visit to the pavement cafés in Melville. The fashion-conscious hang out in Nelson Mandela Square or Rivonia Road, or visit the antique shops and cafés of Parkhurst.

Surprisingly for such a large, densely populated city, there are many nature

THE LIBERATION STRUGGLE

Although it was formed in 1912, the ANC only resorted to taking up arms after it was banned by the state in 1960. Initially, most military actions took the form of sabotage of power lines and other infrastructures. In the 1970s and 1980s, however, armed guerrillas sometimes clashed with security forces and carried out bomb attacks against both strategic and civilian targets.

As the nationwide civil unrest of the 1980s intensified, ANC supporters also clashed with those of the Inkatha Freedom Party and others perceived to be supporters of the state. Troops and riot police patrolled the townships almost constantly from 1984 and clashed with ANC supporting youths on a daily basis. This violence continued until the early 1990s, even after Mandela was released.

Eponymous bronze statue in Nelson Mandela Square, Sandton

reserves. At the Walter Sisulu National Botanical Gardens, carefully tended displays of plants from all over South Africa thrive, while on the cliffs above the rolling lawns a pair of wild black eagles continue to breed, as they have done for more than a decade.

Apartheid Museum

A plethora of multimedia displays take the visitor through the stark cruelty of racial separation enforced by apartheid, but also showcase South Africa's remarkable transition to democracy. The story is skilfully told, and provides an invaluable insight into the development of modern South Africa. *Gold Reef Rd, Crown Mines. Tel: (011) 309 4700. www.apartheidmuseum.org. Open: Tue–Sun 10am–5pm. Closed:*

Mon, Good Friday & Christmas Day. Admission charge.

Constitution Hill

South Africa's new Constitutional Court has been built here around the notorious former prison called The Fort. Many famous prisoners, including Nelson Mandela and Mahatma Gandhi, were once held in the prison. Various parts of the prison are used as galleries explaining the history of The Fort.
Constitution Hill, Braamfontein. Tel: (011) 381 3100. www.constitutionhill.org.za. Open: daily 9am–5pm, hourly tours. Admission charge.

Gold Reef City

The theme park has been built around an authentic 19th-century gold mine. Visitors can travel 200m (650ft) underground down a mine to learn about the industry and the history of South Africa's biggest gold rush. Various other forms of entertainment are offered, including 'gumboot dancing' made famous by migrant mine-workers. There are amusement park rides and a hotel and casino nearby.
Crown Mines. Tel: (011) 248 6800. www.goldreefcity.co.za. Open: Wed–Sun & school holidays daily 9.30am–5pm. Admission charge.

Johannesburg Art Gallery

This large gallery has one of the country's best art collections. Works

Apartheid Museum, Johannesburg

include those by local and international artists, both contemporary and classical. There are also many collections of local beadwork, carving and other exhibits.
Joubert Park. Tel: (011) 725 3130. www.joburg.org.za. Open: Tue–Sun 10am–5pm. Closed: Mon. Free admission. It is best to visit with a tour guide as the Joubert Park area is unsafe for tourists.

Markets

Over 500 stalls at the **Rosebank Mall Rooftop Market** offer crafts, artworks, books, clothing and food. The market is particularly good for African carvings, masks, figurines and jewellery. Food is available too.

The Bruma Fleamarket offers a wide variety of goods, including African artwork, carvings and other curios. As with the Rosebank Mall Rooftop Market, bargaining is acceptable and expected. There are food stalls, and at weekends and holidays there is entertainment too, often in the form of traditional dancers.

Rosebank Mall Rooftop Market.
www.themallofrosebank.co.za.
Open: Sun 9am–5pm.
Bruma Fleamarket.
Corner Marcia Ave and Ernest Oppenheimer St, Bruma.
Tel: (011) 622 9648.
Open: Tue–Sun 9.30am–5pm.

Museum Africa

This is Johannesburg's major cultural history museum and is housed in the old Market Building, which was built in 1913. Permanent exhibitions include displays of South African rock art, geology, and photography dating back 100 years.

The dangers of mining and the rise of township jazz are among several themes highlighted. The 'Tried for Treason' display tells the story of Nelson Mandela and 155 other prisoners who went on trial in 1956 for their anti-apartheid activities.

121 Bree St, Newtown.
Tel: (011) 833 5624.
Open: Tue–Sun 9am–5pm. Closed: Mon. Small admission charge.

Sandton

Sandton City, **Nelson Mandela Square** and the nearby **Hyde Park Corner**

Inside Rosebank Mall market

Shopping Centre form the heart of the wealthy shopping areas of the lush northern suburbs. African fashion and influences rub shoulders with imports directly from Europe. The season's trends and famous labels are all important to well-heeled shoppers browsing the boutiques.

A range of upmarket cafés provide useful vantage points to watch who is buying what, and good bookshops and cinemas offer somewhat more cerebral relaxation.

Sandton City. 5th St, Sandton.
Tel: (011) 217 6000.
www.sandtoncity.com. Open: Mon–Sat 9am–6pm, Sun 10am–4pm.
Nelson Mandela Square. 5th St, Sandton.
Tel: (011) 217 6000.
www.nelsonmandelasquare.com.
Open: daily 9am–6pm.

Hyde Park Corner Shopping Centre.
Jan Smuts Ave. Tel: (011) 325 4340.
www.hydeparkshopping.co.za.
Open: Mon–Sat 9am–6pm, Sun
10am–1pm.

South African Lipizzaners

These powerful white 'dancing horses' are famed for their skill in executing complex movements in the classical traditions invented by Spanish riding masters during the Middle Ages. The Kyalami Centre is the only riding school outside of the Spanish Riding School in Vienna, Austria, with official approval to conduct Lipizzaner performances.

There are 65 of these rare horses based at Kyalami, and every Sunday expert riders put the stallions through their complex routines.
1 Dahlia Rd, Kyalami.
Tel: (011) 702 2103.
www.lipizzaners.co.za.
Shows: Sun 10.30am.
Admission charge.

The financial district in Johannesburg

South African National Museum of Military History

This museum contains a unique collection of weaponry and uniforms spanning 120 years of South African military history, including the Anglo-Zulu War, the South African War, World Wars I and II and the liberation wars fought during the birth of modern South Africa.

The displays include artillery pieces, tanks and other armoured vehicles, a German-made, two-man mini-submarine and the only preserved World War II Messerschmitt Me 260 B jet night fighter.

Herman Ekstein Park (close to the Johannesburg Zoo), entrance intersection Erlswold and Eastwold Ave, Saxonwold. Tel: (011) 646 5513. www.militarymuseum.co.za. Open: daily 9.30am–4.30pm. Admission charge.

Soweto

The vibrant, dusty streets of Soweto provide a fascinating insight into the complex world of South African society. Built by apartheid's planners merely to provide labour for industry, Soweto and other townships have a life and culture of their own, and are a world apart from the Western orientation of Johannesburg's more affluent areas.

Much of the struggle against apartheid took place in areas like Soweto, and there are several memorials to those who died, including the Hector Peterson Memorial in Orlando West.

Most tours take in these memorials as well as the former homes of two Nobel Peace Prize winners, Nelson Mandela and Archbishop Desmond Tutu. Both homes are in Vilakazi Street, the only street in the world that can boast two Nobel Prize winners.

The sprawling township of Soweto

Elsewhere, visitors get a flavour of township life, visiting small restaurants or *shebeens* (bars).

Taking an organised tour is advised, and several operators run tours to Soweto, Alexandra and other townships (www.gauteng.net).

Walter Sisulu National Botanical Gardens

This 300-hectare (740-acre) area features a variety of walks through the landscaped and natural *veld* areas, which showcase many species of indigenous plants. Over 230 species of birds have been recorded, as well as a number of small mammals. The 70m (230ft)-high Witpoortjie Falls is visible from most parts of the gardens, which also include a small dam and bird hide.

Open-air concerts are held in winter, when the sun is still warm, but rain is

Walter Sisulu National Botanical Gardens, near Johannesburg

REGINA MUNDI CHURCH

Regina Mundi, sometimes known as 'The Queen of Soweto', is a church that has played a pivotal role in the township's turbulent political history.

During the apartheid years, the huge Catholic Church, which can seat 2,000 people, was often used as a venue for political gatherings, many of which were disrupted by police using tear gas and, in some instances, guns. During the 1976 Soweto uprisings, children wounded by police gunfire took refuge in the church, as did many others in later years.

Today, the church, built in 1964, has had a park created in its gardens, and inside the church there is an art gallery featuring the history of Soweto and Johannesburg.

unlikely, and many bring picnics and sit on the rolling lawns while listening to the music.

Malcolm Rd, Poortview, Roodepoort. Tel: (086) 100 1278. www.sanbi.org. Open: 8am–6pm all year. Admission charge.

Pretoria

Pretoria is South Africa's capital but, despite its political importance, this small city moves at a relatively leisurely pace. The city has been the seat of various South African governments for most of the last 110 years, beginning with the Boer Republics, which declared independence from Britain in the late 1800s, and most recently the African National Congress-controlled government.

As the home of the country's civil service and international diplomatic corps, it is a fairly staid city, although vibrant pockets of restaurants and clubs keep students and more adventurous officials up until the early hours. The University of Pretoria is one of South Africa's largest, and is known for its wildlife and, in particular, mammal research, and the nearby Transvaal Museum has important collections of a wide range of species.

Various museums and art galleries reflect much of South Africa's past, but also illustrate the constantly developing nature of the country's social and political structure. At the start of the hot summers, much of the city becomes covered in the purple blossom of the jacaranda trees that line many of the wide streets.

Ditsong Museum of Natural History

This museum has one of the best collections of southern African birds, mammals, insects and reptiles in the country.

The displays provide a complete overview of nearly all the species most people are likely to see. A wide range of lectures and presentations are offered throughout the year, and special programmes for children are also available.

It is a working museum, and research staff contribute significantly to the knowledge pool of many species on a regular basis.

Paul Kruger St, Pretoria.

The Union Buildings in Pretoria are the seat of the South African government

Tel: (012) 322 7632.
www.ditsong.org.za. Open: daily
8am–4pm. Closed: Christmas Day &
Good Friday.

Melrose House

Set in verdant gardens, this museum
was originally a Victorian home built in
1886. Later it became the headquarters
of the British forces fighting against the
Boers in the South African War of
1899–1902.

Throughout the latter years of the
war, generals briefed Queen Victoria
from the house, and in 1902 the Treaty
of Vereeniging was signed here, ending
the conflict.

The architecture of the house and
displays of furniture and other bric-a-
brac provide a good example of the
tastes of wealthy Victorian colonial
settlers. Displays of period
photographs reveal the harsh
conditions of this war.
275 Jacob Maré St, Pretoria.
Tel: (012) 322 0420.
www.melrosehouse.co.za.
Open: Tue–Sun 10am–5pm.
Closed: Mon. Admission charge.

Pretoria Art Museum

This important museum has fine
examples of many forms of South
African art, including contemporary
work as well as that of older, more
established artists.

South Africa's best-known 'old
school' painters such as Anton van
Wouw, Maggie Loubser, Jacob Hendrik

The Ditsong Museum of Natural History is
South Africa's leading natural history museum

Pierneef and Irma Stern are exhibited,
and many prints and other media from
the 18th and 19th centuries are also
displayed. The gallery highlights the
transition of modern South African art
away from a purely Eurocentric base,
and also emphasises the use of more
unorthodox media.
218 Vermeulen St.
Tel: (012) 344 1807.
www.pretoriaartmuseum.co.za.
Open: Tue–Sun 10am–5pm.
Closed: Mon & public holidays.
Admission charge.

The Union Buildings

Designed by the famous British colonial
architect Sir Herbert Baker, and
completed in 1913, the Union Buildings

have loomed large in the minds of South Africans ever since.

For a long time the seat of the apartheid government, these sandstone buildings represented to many the oppression of apartheid rule. In 1994, it was here that Nelson Mandela was sworn in as president.

Perched on a hill, the buildings and surrounding gardens provide good views of the city.

Tours of the gardens can be arranged Mon–Fri. Contact local tour operators (see Directory on p189).

Voortrekker Monument

Just outside Pretoria the huge granite Voortrekker Monument is visible for kilometres, and commemorates the spirit of the Voortrekkers who left the Cape in 1834. The monument also depicts a belief that God supported them in their various battles.

Tel: (012) 326 6770.
www.voortrekkermon.org.za.
Open: daily 9am–4.30pm.
Admission charge.

Further afield in Gauteng
Chameleon Village Lifestyle Junxion

A huge range of African arts and crafts are available from both the formal and informal markets here. Weekends are busy as there are many tourists and locals on their way to Sun City (*see pp102–3*), or just enjoying a day in the sun shopping for bargains. Traders come from as far afield as Kenya, Senegal and the Democratic Republic

of the Congo, and some of the goods on sale reflect their origins.

The market is at the foot of Commando Nek mountain pass, near the Hartebeespoort Dam wall. It is 25 minutes from Pretoria and about 50 minutes from Johannesburg. It is a good place to stop while on the way to Sun City or the Pilanesberg National Park (see p102). Tel: (012) 253 1451. www.chameleonvillage.co.za

Cradle of Humankind

The area of rocky grass- and shrub-covered hills and valleys some 45 minutes north of central Johannesburg has proved to be one of the most important hominid fossil sites in the world.

Already more than 500 hominid fossils and 9,000 stone tools have been uncovered, including an almost complete 2.6 million-year-old *Australopithecine* skull fondly known as 'Mrs Ples'.

There are 12 distinct sites scattered along the Sterkfontein Valley, including the Sterkfontein Cave, Wonder Caves and Swartkrans where there is evidence of the earliest known deliberate use of fire about 1.3 million years ago.

Various operators run tours to the Cradle and there is an excellent restaurant nearby.

Maropeng Visitor Centre.
Off R400 highway. Tel: (014) 577 9000.
www.maropeng.co.za.
Sterkfontein Caves Visitor Centre.
Tel: (011) 668 3200.
www.maropeng.co.za.
Admission charge.

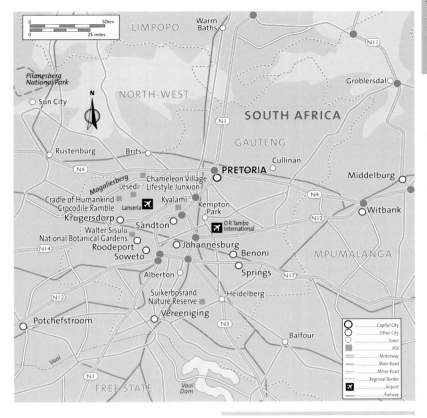

Crocodile Ramble

This area borders on the Magaliesberg region, and there are dozens of art galleries, craft shops, cafés and hotels. Many people from both Johannesburg and Pretoria spend a Saturday or Sunday wandering around various parts of the Ramble area shopping or having tea or lunch. Contact the Ramble tourism office for an electronic or print brochure. Events and exhibitions change regularly. The area also borders on the Cradle of Humankind (*see p94*).

CASINOS

Although a relatively new phenomenon in South Africa (they were outlawed prior to 1994), casinos are hugely popular, and the spinning wheels and bright lights attract thousands of hopeful customers daily.

The casinos and accompanying hotels tend to be situated near the larger cities, but operate in all of the nine provinces. Some of the larger casinos are part of big shopping complexes or have other attractions, including amusement parks, nearby.

South Africa also has a national lottery. It is known as The Lotto, for which winners are selected every Wednesday and Saturday.

Hartebeespoort Dam, west of Pretoria

Tel: (086) 172 6253.
www.theramble.co.za

Cullinan

The largest diamond ever found, the whopping 3,106-carat Cullinan diamond, was found here in 1905. Still a rich source of diamonds, the mine offers regular tours where the mining process – from digging the first hole to cutting the final gem – is explained.

The village has many well-preserved homes and buildings and various museum stores and quiet restaurants help complete a morning or afternoon visit. The village is about 60km (37 miles) east of Pretoria.
Cullinan Tourism. Tel: (012) 734 2170. www.cullinanmeander.co.za. Mine tours: Mon–Fri.

Lesedi Cultural Village

Typical Xhosa, Zulu, Pedi and Basotho homesteads have been built within the village where visitors experience something of the scope and feel of the many traditional cultures that make up South Africa. Guides explain some of the intricacies of each culture, and audiovisual displays are also used.

Dancers later entertain tourists while lunch is served. A variety of curios and artwork is available, as is overnight accommodation.
See the website for directions. About 45 minutes from Johannesburg and 25 minutes from Pretoria.
Tel: (012) 205 1394. www.lesedi.com. Tours: daily 11.30am & 4.30pm. Admission charge.

Magaliesberg mountains

Many residents of nearby Pretoria and Johannesburg escape the cities at the weekend to enjoy outdoor pursuits in the rolling countryside near the high southerly facing cliffs of the Magaliesberg mountains, which run for some 100km (60 miles) east of Pretoria.

Many B&Bs and country lodges are scattered throughout the region, and innumerable stalls and shops offer crafts, country food and other local products.

Horse riding, hiking, camping and birdwatching are just some of the outdoor attractions which attract day-trippers, although others simply visit the area for a quiet weekend lunch and a bit of casual shopping. The Magaliesberg are easily accessible from both Johannesburg and Pretoria.
Magaliesberg Tourism.
Tel: (014) 577 0060.
www.magaliesberg.co.za

Suikerbosrand Nature Reserve

High grass-covered hills and rocky stream valleys give visitors an idea of what the area around Johannesburg would have looked like before the city developed.

A surprising amount of small game including antelope occurs in the 13,337-hectare (32,950-acre) reserve, which is near the town of Heidelberg, some 45km (28 miles) from the centre of Johannesburg. Hiking trails, a circular drive and picnic sites can be found here.

Johannesburg and the surrounding urban sprawl are visible from the northern side of the reserve and provide a sobering reminder of how much humans have changed our planet. *Tel: (011) 904 3930. www.gauteng.net. Open: all year.*

Gauteng

A wide range of soapstone and wooden carvings is sold by roadside vendors

Free State

The Free State is a quiet agricultural province where everything moves along at a sedate rural pace. Even the citizens of the capital city Bloemfontein don't pay too much attention to the world rushing by – they're too happy enjoying the nearby wide open spaces and blue skies. Most tourists head for the mountainous southeast, but there are rewarding cultural sites, museums and other attractions all over the province.

Bloemfontein

In Afrikaaans, Bloemfontein means 'flower spring'. Today the town has grown into the largest city in the Free State. There are several museums and monuments, but the most significant is the National Women's Memorial and War Museum commemorating the 26,000 Boer women and children who died in British concentration camps during the Second Boer War of 1899–1902.
*Mangaung/Bloemfontein Visitor Information Centre.
Tel: (051) 412 7940.
www.bloemfontein.co.za*

Freshford House

A restored house dating from 1897, this museum offers a snapshot of everyday life in Bloemfontein at the turn of the 20th century.
*31 Kellner St. Tel: (051) 447 9609.
www. nasmus.co.za. Open: Mon–Fri 10am–1pm, Sat & Sun 2–5pm.
Admission charge.*

National Museum

This museum focuses on the natural and cultural environment, and exhibits include life-size fibreglass elephants.
Corner Charles St and Aliwal St. Tel: (051) 447 9609. www.nasmus.co.za. Open: Mon–Fri 8am–5pm, Sat 10am–5pm, Sun noon–5.30pm. Admission charge.

National Women's Memorial and War Museum of the Boer Republics
Monument Rd. Tel: (051) 447 3447. www.anglo-boer.co.za. Open: Mon–Fri 8am–4.30pm, Sat 10am–5pm, Sun 11am–5pm. Admission charge.

Clarens

Wide-open grasslands and maize fields give way to mountains and sandstone bluffs near the pretty village of Clarens close to the Lesotho border. It has become an artists' haven, and galleries have sprung up all over town.

The clear, cold streams and mountain air make for good biking, horse riding, hiking and trout fishing.

Clarens Publicity Association.
Tel: (058) 256 1542.
www.clarenstourism.co.za

Golden Gate Highlands National Park

Set in among sandstone mountains with crystal-clear streams and dams, the park offers excellent walking, hiking and horse riding. San hunters used to shelter here, and a variety of grassland game species still occur.

The park is very close to Clarens and it is worth visiting both. The former QwaQwa National Park (now part of the Golden Gate Highlands National Park) is undeveloped, with good mountain scenery. There is a Basotho cultural village, depicting traditional life.
South African National Parks Central Reservations. Tel: (012) 428 9111.
www.sanparks.org.
The Sterkfontein Dam Nature Reserve is nearby.

Train journeys

South Africa is one of the few remaining countries where you can still experience magical railway journeys in trains of enormous prestige. Make an epic journey conjuring up the romance of a lost age of steam travel, or take a short trip for just a day out or a weekend away.

UNDER STEAM
The epic journey
Rovos Rail The magnificently restored, privately owned Pride of Africa travels a variety of routes. From Cape Town, destinations include Victoria Falls (Zimbabwe) and Dar es Salaam (Tanzania), with stopovers at Matjiesfontein, Kimberley and Pretoria, and optional sightseeing en route.

Sleepers, dining car and observation carriages are the refurbished originals, a reminder of pre-war opulence.
Tel: (012) 315 8242.
www.rovos.co.za

Shongololo Express Named after a local millipede, this service offers luxurious train rides taking in all the highlights of South Africa from Kruger National Park to Cape Town. The trains also travel to eight other southern African countries. Choose from three 8-day and three 16-day tours.
Tel: (011) 483 0657.
www.shongololo.com

Union Limited A steam locomotive and original carriages of the old Union Limited – the first luxury train (1923) taking first-class passengers from Johannesburg to Cape Town to meet the ocean liners – have been transformed into a 'safari' train with a variety of routes and destinations.
Tel: (021) 449 4391.
Email: steamsa@transnet.co.za.
Call to confirm schedule.

Short excursions
Friends of the Rail This railway heritage association runs regular steam train day trips from Hermanstad Station in Pretoria to the historic diamond-mining town of Cullinan, as well as looped trips around Pretoria – a good day out.
Tel: (082) 098 6186.
www.friendsoftherail.com

Magaliesberg Express The South African National Railway and Steam Museum Preservation Group offers day trips from Johannesburg Station to the Magaliesberg mountains (*see p96*).

First Sunday of every month from Johannesburg's Park Station.

Magaliesberg Tourism
Tel: (012) 888 1154.
www.magaliesberg.co.za.
Call to confirm schedule.

Die Herrie Operating between Oudtshoorn and Calitzdorp, the train traverses ostrich country and the Karoo.
Tel: (044) 272 2377.
Call to confirm schedule.

Outeniqua Choo-Tjoe This distinguished old steam train covers the George to Mossel Bay section of the Garden Route (*see Garden Route feature on pp66–9*), and is probably one of the country's most enjoyable services, passing through spectacular scenery.
Tel: (044) 801 8202.
www.outeniquachootjoe.co.za.
Mon–Sat, but call to confirm schedule. 4–6 hour round trip.

The Apple Express The Apple Express runs from Port Elizabeth, and crosses the historic Van Staden's river bridge, the highest narrow-gauge railway bridge in the world.
Tel: (082) 921 8512.
www.apple-express.co.za

DIESEL OR ELECTRIC TRAIN TRAVEL

The Blue Train

The Blue Train replaced the old Johannesburg–Cape Town Union Limited train in 1939. Its name derives from the colour of the original train.

Today's Blue Train is one of the great trains of the world. It may be a slower alternative to flying (Cape Town to Pretoria takes 24 hours), but it's an infinitely superior experience. It has sleeping accommodation with showers, a dining and lounge car, and space to carry cars.

The train runs between Cape Town and Pretoria and from Pretoria to the Pilanesberg Game Reserve (known as the Bakubung Special).
Tel: (012) 334 8459 (Pretoria) or (021) 449 2672 (Cape Town).
www.bluetrain.co.za

Regular passenger services

Regular intercity trains traverse some amazing landscapes. The best routes are the Trans-Karoo, the Trans-Orange, the Trans-KZN and the Algoa Express. There are a variety of discounts for children and senior citizens.

Visit *www.shosholoza-meyl.co.za* for further information on services to Johannesburg, Durban, Cape Town, Port Elizabeth, Kimberley and East London, among others.

North West

The Pilanesberg and Madikwe Game Reserves and the Sun City golf course and entertainment complex are the tourism hubs of this rural province. All three destinations are close enough to Johannesburg and Pretoria for quick visits. Both game reserves are relatively small and have thriving populations of the 'Big Five' and other animals, which usually ensures good game viewing. Platinum mining, farming and tourism are the major economic activities of the province.

Pilanesberg National Park

Situated in the eroded remains of a huge 1,300 million-year-old volcano crater, this park provides the closest 'Big Five' game-viewing to Johannesburg and Pretoria, which are about two hours away by road. The reserve was formed with the purchase of cattle farms in the 1970s and restocked with wild game, one of the largest operations of its kind ever undertaken. A network

Game Viewing Hide, Mankwe Dam, Pilanesberg National Park

of good asphalt and gravel roads suitable for normal cars and the large numbers of animal usually ensure good game viewing. The drivers of private game vehicles zipping around the park are all in touch with each other via radio, and are usually happy to give sighting tips to other visitors. Apart from the prolific wildlife, the landscapes in Pilanesberg are varied and beautiful when compared to other parks. Make sure to drive up to the Lenong viewpoint from where the concentric circles of the old crater are clearly visible. A wide range of accommodation is available inside or just outside the park, both in deluxe private camps and the more affordable Bakgatla and Manyane rest-camps run by Golden Leopard Resorts, which have comfortable chalets, tents, camping, restaurants and swimming pools. The Sun City complex with several hotels is near the southernmost Bakubung Gate. Weekends can be very busy due to the park's proximity to the cities in

Gauteng and the guests at Sun City, but entering the park at the crack of dawn and lingering till near closing time ensures some quiet hours and the greatest chance of seeing shy animals. *170km (105 miles) west of Johannesburg. Tel: (014) 555 1600. www.pilanesberg-game-reserve.co.za. Open: all year round.*

Sun City

This complex of hotels, casinos and golf courses is South Africa's answer to Las Vegas. The expensive Lost City complex is a fantasyland of carved animals and an opulent, palace-like hotel. The older Sun City has similar, if less grand, facilities and the Valley of the Waves water attraction provides a seaside experience for children, complete with artificially generated breakers, hundreds of kilometres from the nearest ocean.

Both complexes have world-class golf courses, and in December, some of the world's best players compete here for a vast amount of prize money.

The complex is on the borders of the Pilanesberg National Park. *Tel: (011) 557 1000. www.suninternational.com*

Madikwe Game Reserve

This is another game reserve that used to be cattle farms, now restocked with game, including the 'Big Five'. It is also malaria-free. Although self-drive visits are not allowed, there are several lodges in the reserve, and

18th hole at Sun City golf course

all offer day and night drives with trained guides.

The area is hot in summer and has mild winter days. *Tel: (018) 3672 and ask for 2411.*

RESERVE LODGES

Golden Leopard Resorts
Tel: (014) 555 1000.
www.goldenleopardresorts.co.za
The Bush House
www.madikwe-game-reserve.co.za
Etali Safari Lodge
www.etalisafari.co.za
Jaci's Safari Lodge
www.madikwe.com
Madikwe River Lodge
www.madikweriverlodge.com
Mateya Safari Lodge
www.mateyasafari.co.za
Mosetlha Bush Camp
www.thebushcamp.com
Tau Game Lodge
www.taugamelodge.co.za

Mpumalanga

Kruger National Park is Mpumalanga's most famous attraction, but the province also has some of the best trout fishing in South Africa, many smaller game parks and wonderful scenery. Just over 120 years ago, the hills around Barberton and Pilgrim's Rest were the focus of a frenzied gold rush. Museums in many towns exhibit memories of the Second Boer War (1899–1902). Shangaan culture is also highlighted in several art galleries and cultural villages.

Barberton

Barberton was founded after the discovery of gold. Its fame, however, was short-lived, as the far richer finds on the Witwatersrand caused an almost immediate exodus of fortune-seekers. Many of the town's old buildings survived, including the Kaap Gold Fields' Stock Exchange, the Transvaal's first stock exchange, and the 1887 Globe Tavern, a hostelry of a type common in the goldfields of the late 19th century.

The Barberton Museum contains artefacts relating to the gold-rush days. In Barberton Park, there is a statue of the dog Jock, the subject of Sir Percy FitzPatrick's famous story, *Jock of the Bushveld*. Many people hike or ride horses in the hills around Barberton.
Barberton Information Bureau.
Tel: (013) 712 2880.
www.barberton.co.za

Dullstroom

Dullstroom has become a trendy weekend getaway destination, and is the centre of the thriving trout-fishing industry. Many people visit the area simply to walk in the hills and to spend a quiet weekend at one of the wide range of guest farms or lodges. Others pursue the brown and rainbow trout with passion. A wide range of craft shops and restaurants has been established in the village and surrounding areas.

Nearby, Lydenberg is also an important fly-fishing area.
Dullstroom Accommodation.
Tel: (013) 254 0020.
www.dullstroom.co.za

Barberton in Mpumalanga

The gold-rush-era village of Pilgrim's Rest is now a national monument

Hazyview
Shangana Cultural Village

Dressed in traditional skins and headdresses, Shangana dancers and storytellers recount some of the legends of their people and region at this village close to the borders of Kruger National Park. Curios made by local people are also sold at the Marula Market in the village.

Hazyview. Tel: (013) 737 5804/5.
www.shangana.co.za.
Open: daily, but contact them for performance times.

Nelspruit and White River

Nelspruit is the largest town and capital of Mpumalanga. It is also the gateway to the Lowveld.

The **Lowveld National Botanical Gardens** are well worth visiting, and have an impressive collection of cycads and other Lowveld flowers and trees.

Nearby is the subtropical town of White River where mangos, avocados and other fruit are grown. Soon after White River, the orchards begin to make way for game-ranching land.
Lowveld National Botanical Gardens.
Tel: (013) 752 5531.
www.sanbi.org

Sudwala Caves

Northwest of Nelspruit on the slopes of the Northern Drakensberg are the Sudwala Caves. Visitors are only allowed to pass through the first few hundred metres, and the total depth of the cavern system is still uncertain.

Within the caves are bizarre rock formations, spectacular stalactites and stalagmites, and fossils of prehistoric algae. Below the entrance to the caves there is a restaurant and an open-air museum with life-size replicas of dinosaurs and other prehistoric creatures.

Mpumalanga Tourism Authority.
Tel: (013) 759 5300.
www.mpumalanga.com

Kruger National Park

Pretoriuskop Camp in Kruger National Park

Sprawling across a vast expanse of hot, game-rich bush and woodland, intersected by four major rivers and bordered by two others, is Kruger National Park. The park is one of Africa's premier wildlife areas and tourist destinations; a vital component in southern African and worldwide conservation, Kruger attracts more than a million visitors a year. The park covers some 20,000sq km (7,722sq miles), and there are 25 camps offering many types of accommodation. There are several top-of-the-range, privately run lodges too. Each rest camp offers something different in the way of scenery, and the game and birdlife varies according to habitat.

The view from the Olifants thatched camp, high on the hill overlooking the Olifants River, is spectacular. Visitors get eye-level views of circling marabou storks and vultures, while far below elephants browse among the knob thorn and mopane trees.

Further south, near Skukuza, the largest camp in the park, wild dogs are often spotted, and lucky visitors sometimes see these rare predators hunting, their white-tipped tails streaming behind them as they chase their quarry through the bush. Almost 500 species of bird occur in the park. Animal guidebooks must be large to cover the huge variety of mammals, reptiles, trees and insects.

The area covered by Kruger also has a rich human history. Near Pafuri, the stone citadel of Thulamela, which has now been restored to its former glory, dates back to the Late Iron Age. It was an important cultural and trading settlement with links to other stone cities like Great Zimbabwe.

Recently, fences between Kruger National Park and a conservation area in neighbouring Mozambique have been taken down, enabling the formation of the Great Limpopo Transfrontier Park. Similarly, fences have been taken down along the western boundary of Kruger National Park. This allows the free movement of game from well-run, upmarket private game reserves developed along the park's boundary.

Kruger tips:

- If you are on a self-drive trip in Kruger National Park, plan your day carefully. Distances are considerable, and game viewing takes time.

- All camp gates are locked at last light and only opened again at daybreak.

- The speed limit on tar roads is 50kph (30mph), and on gravel roads it is 40kph (25mph). Authorities set up speed traps and issue fines in an attempt to control speeding. Cars kill hundreds of wild animals and birds annually.

- In summer, it is best to get up at first light and travel in the cool of the morning. Return to camp for a brunch and siesta in the middle of the day, when the temperatures can climb dramatically. Go out on another game drive after 3pm.

- Make sure to book a night drive with a trained guide – private individuals are not allowed to drive outside the camps at night.

- Talk to other guests and park staff about game sightings. It will help you plan your viewing, although there is no guarantee that the animals will be in the same place.

- Take adequate supplies of food and drink with you when you set off on a drive.

Kruger National Park is home to approximately 1,500 lions

The 'Big Five'

The 'Big Five' are the trump cards of African game reserves. Everyone wants to see them. The 'Big Five' are the lion, elephant, rhinoceros, leopard and buffalo. The term has an unfortunate origin – to early hunters these were considered to be the most dangerous animals to kill, and in some instances, the hunters did become the hunted, with fatal consequences.

Today, these animals are considered hugely important in the tourism industry, and have status that would have shocked people 100 years ago. In many instances, they were considered to be, at best, pests and, in some cases, vermin.

Be wary of a short-tempered buffalo

African buffalo

Although they may look like large, docile cows, buffalo can be extremely aggressive and often drive off lions attacking a herd member. Lone bulls are notoriously short tempered, and walking through thick bush when they are around can be a nerve-racking experience. They weigh between 700–800kg (1,540–1,760lb).

Elephant

Elephants are the second most popular animals among visitors to Africa. Male elephants are huge, and some mature bulls weigh over 6,500kg (14,300lb) and stand about 3.3m (10ft 9in) at the shoulder. Females are considerably smaller.

They are entirely vegetarian and eat leaves, fruit, bark, grass and other vegetable matter. They have a considerable impact on their environment due to their habit of pushing over trees to get at succulent new leaves and twigs. Female matriarchs lead all herds, but mature bulls visit regularly to mate.

Leopard

Leopards are usually secretive animals and sometimes live close to human settlements for years without being

Leopards are beautiful and solitary animals

detected. These solitary carnivores are remarkably strong for their size. Males weigh about 80–90kg (176–198lb), and hunt by sight and hearing. They are quite capable of killing animals much larger than themselves.

Leopards are exceptionally patient hunters and will spend long periods crouching motionless while watching their prey. These spotted cats are extremely beautiful, and once seen in the wild are seldom forgotten.

Lion

Research shows that tourists like to watch these animals more than any other species. They are the only communal large cats and live in prides that sometimes exceed 20 animals.

Large males weigh over 200kg (440lb) and females average around 130kg (286lb). They often hunt cooperatively, some animals flushing prey and others making the kill.

Popular myth has it that males simply eat whatever lionesses kill, but the reality is that they are fearsome predators and often kill for themselves. They usually hunt under cover of darkness.

Rhinoceros

Two species, the black and the white, occur in southern Africa. The white rhino is the larger of the two – bulls weigh up to 2,600kg (5,730lb) – whereas the black rhino seldom weighs more than 1,200kg (2,645lb). Black rhinos have a reputation for being bad tempered and charging without warning, but they usually only do so when they feel threatened.

The black rhino is endangered, with only about 3,300 individuals left in the wild and captivity worldwide.

Lions are particularly well protected at Kruger National Park

Tour: Blyde River Canyon

This tour winds through the Northern Drakensberg mountains, and takes in a series of spectacular vistas of the mountains and the Lowveld far below. Along the way, there are many opportunities to stop for a snack or to shop.

The tour is suitable for a self-drive trip, although several companies offer tours that follow a similar route.

Allow a full day. Start at Sabie, and head north past Graskop along the edge of the escarpment on the R37, and then along the R532 to the Blyde River Canyon.

1 Sabie and Graskop

The pleasant village of Sabie is the centre of a thriving commercial forestry industry. There are several high

An old miner's house has been converted into a shop at Pilgrim's Rest

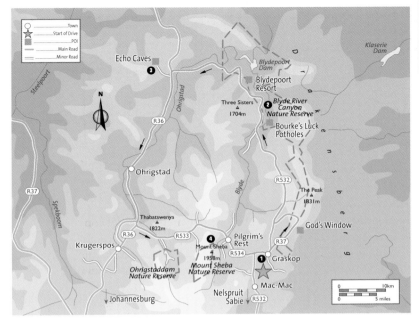

waterfalls in the area, including the Bridal Veil Falls (70m/230ft), the Lone Creek Falls (68m/223ft) and the Mac Mac Falls (64m/210ft) near Graskop.

The Forestry Museum in Sabie tells the story of the lumber industry in the area. Graskop, 29km (18 miles) to the north, was once a gold-mining settlement, but is today also closely linked to the forestry industry and tourism. Be sure to stop and enjoy the magnificent view of the Blyde River Canyon from the God's Window viewpoint north of Graskop. *Beyond God's Window, the R532 continues past the Bourke's Luck Potholes, which have been ground into the rock by the swirling waters. There are viewing platforms here.*

The road continues to the Blyde River Canyon Nature Reserve.

Lisbon Falls, north of Graskop

2 Blyde River Canyon Nature Reserve

The Blyde River gouges its way through the mountains, and has created a 20km (12-mile)-long canyon that is 800m (2,600ft) deep in places. There are any number of panoramic views here, and dominating the area are three peaks known as the Three Sisters (also known as the Three Rondavels). The Lisbon and Berlin Falls are nearby. There is a wide variety of hiking trails that wind along the face of the mountains.

From Blydepoort, the road heads north to the junction of the R36. Turn left here towards Ohrigstad. Close to the junction is the road to the Echo Caves.

Roadside hawkers often sell animal carvings

3 Echo Caves

The sequence of chambers in the Molopong Valley has yielded a rich collection of Middle and Late Stone Age implements. There is an open-air display of archaeological implements.

ROADSIDE HAWKERS

In many parts of South Africa, hawkers sell curios and other goods at the roadside. Many offer prices much lower than established shops. It is, however, wise to check wooden carvings, especially the larger items, for cracks or splits. In some cases, shoe polish is used to hide the cracks.

Many of the carvings, particularly those of giraffes, are designed to stand, but check the bases to make sure they are flat. In some cases they may seem perfectly fine at the roadside but are, in reality, craftily supported with stones or sticks.

Follow the R36 to Ohrigstad and then take the R533 to Pilgrim's Rest.

4 Pilgrim's Rest

This entire village has been declared a national monument. It was the scene of a gold rush after Alec 'Wheelbarrow' Patterson found alluvial deposits of the precious metal here in 1887. Much of the town has been preserved in its original state, and the main road is lined with red and white corrugated-iron buildings.

The post office building and other museums house memorabilia of the gold-rush era. Many of the shops in the town sell curios and artwork.

Pilgrim's Rest Tourist Information. Tel: (013) 768 1060. www.pilgrimsrest.org.za.

Continue on the R533 until it joins the R534 back to Graskop.

The Three Rondavels (huts) in the Blydepoort Nature Reserve

Limpopo

Most people in this province derive their livelihoods from agriculture and the wildlife industry. The northern half of Kruger National Park is in Limpopo, but there are also smaller reserves and private game ranches scattered throughout the province. A lot of the ranches cater for the hunting industry which attracts many foreign clients. Every Easter, more than a million pilgrims visit the Zionist Christian Church headquarters at Moria, near the capital city Polokwane.

Tzaneen and Magoebaskloof

The cold trout streams of the Magoebaskloof Pass drop steeply down to the subtropical mango, avocado pear and litchi farms around Tzaneen. Tzaneen is in a transition zone between the hot Lowveld and cooler Highveld.

The game ranches that border Kruger National Park begin east of Tzaneen, and to the northeast is the Modjadji Forest, where the Modjadji palm, a form of cycad which evolved over 50 million years ago, grows to a height of some 13m (42ft). The area is also home to the Modjaji Rain Queen, a descendant of a 16th-century Karanga princess. People still ply her with gifts to bring good rains.

Soutpansberg

In the far north of the Limpopo Province, the Soutpansberg Mountains form a very biologically diverse zone. The southern slopes are among some of the wettest in South Africa. However, the northern slopes are dry, and soon give way to the plains and the giant baobab trees that are so characteristic of the Limpopo River Valley.

Hiking trails and game viewing dominate activities in this area, which is also an important tropical fruit-farming region.

The Venda people settled here in the 18th century. Many sites in the area are

NDEBELE ART

Their extraordinary art is the single aspect of South Ndebele culture that distinguishes it from that of other Nguni groups. Usually referred to simply as Ndebele, the South Ndebele live for the most part in the Limpopo Highveld, northeast of Pretoria.

From house painting and beadwork to mural painting and the elaborate traditional dress of the women, the Ndebele's striking attention to colour and pattern and their sense of symmetry are unusual. The palette of the original Ndebele house painters was restricted to ochre, natural clays and charcoals. Their beadwork has considerable cultural significance; for example, specific designs and garments are reserved for married women, and others for widows.

Limpopo and Mpumalanga

sacred. At Dzata are ruins of ancient stone structures, and Lake Fundudzi is believed to be the home of a python god.

The Waterberg

For decades, most tourists ignored this rugged region. However, it is now starting to get the attention it deserves.

Although the Marakele National Park is still in the early stages of development, it shares a boundary with the Welgevonden complex of private game reserves and the two form a malaria-free 'Big Five' wildlife area with good game viewing.

Further north, the Lapalala Wilderness has established itself as an excellently run private reserve, and the Touchstone Ranch offers horseback safari among wild game.

Limpopo Tourism and Parks.
Tel: (014) 736 4328.
www.waterberg-tourism.co.za

KwaZulu-Natal

The 3,000m (9,840ft)-high, sometimes snow-covered peaks of the uKhahlamba-Drakensberg mountains in KwaZulu-Natal slope steeply to subtropical, banana tree-fringed beaches less than 200km (125 miles) to the east. Further north along the hot and humid coastline, Africa's southernmost coral reefs shelter a plethora of brightly coloured fish and other sea life. While only a few kilometres inland, the 'Big Five' thrill tourists in some of Africa's oldest game reserves.

The North Coast, South Coast and Durban area offer good surfing, safe bathing and many exciting dive sites. Between the mountains and beaches, the rolling hills and grasslands of the Midlands and surrounding areas provide some of the best agricultural land in South Africa.

The geographical diversity of KwaZulu-Natal is matched by the cultural mix of its residents. Zulu, British and Indian traditions combine to create a vibrant mosaic of cuisine, dress and culture.

KwaZulu-Natal, formerly known simply as Natal, was colonised by the British in the 19th century. The province later saw several wars fought between the settlers and the Zulu, and later the Boers (of Dutch descent).

In the late 19th century, labourers were brought from India to work in the sugar-cane fields. Today, the province has the largest Indian community in the country. Zulu people make up the majority of the population and,

accordingly, their influence in local government and culture is significant.

Many Zulu people live in rural areas and follow a traditional way of life but often move easily between city and country life.

DURBAN

Warm seas, broad beaches and easy access to the province's many attractions make Durban one of South Africa's most important holiday destinations. Over Christmas, the beaches are packed with holidaymakers, but the city's subtropical climate attracts tourists at any time of the year. In the middle of what passes for winter, the city hosts one of the world's top surfing events. Winter daytime temperatures seldom fall below 21°C (70°F), and summer highs often exceed 30°C (86°F).

Culturally, Durban is a vibrant mix of African, European and Indian cultures. Churches, mosques and synagogues rub shoulders with street

KwaZulu-Natal incl. Lesotho and Swaziland

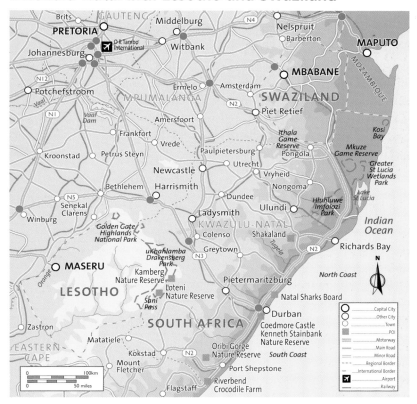

stalls where traditional doctors sell medicines to cure ailments or to ward off evil spirits. As befitting a city with a large Indian population, Durban has become famous in South Africa as the home of hot, spicy curry dishes, but a cosmopolitan range of restaurants provides fare suitable for most palates. Shopping opportunities are nothing if not eclectic, and shops selling the latest electronic goods can be found next to noisy bazaars selling everything from shovels to chicken food.

African Art Centre

Telephone-wire *imbenge* (baskets), beaded wooden or clay animals, ceramics, carvings and other items are made by Zulu and Xhosa women. It is well worth booking a lecture with one or more of the artists who will explain the cultural significance of beadwork and other items.

94 Florida Rd. Tel: (031) 312 3804. www.afriart.org.za. Open: Mon–Fri 8.30am–5pm, Sat 9am–3pm.

Durban

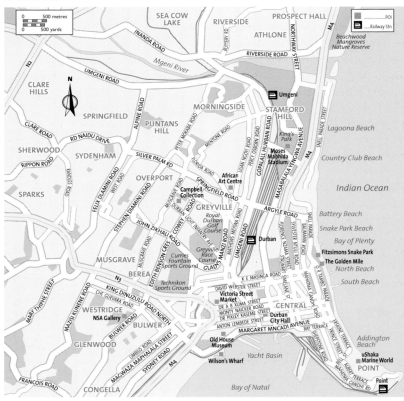

The Campbell Collection

Set on the Berea Ridge overlooking the city, this museum is housed in the Victorian-era Muckelneuk Mansion, former home of sugar baron Sir Marshall Campbell. There is an extensive library of African books, manuscripts and maps. It also contains an important collection of Zulu art, as well as displays of musical instruments, weapons and other items. The Berea provides excellent views of Durban.
220 Gladys Mazibuko Rd, Berea.

Tel: (031) 260 1722.
Viewing and tours by appointment only.

Coedmore Castle and Kenneth Stainbank Nature Reserve

Coedmore Castle was built by the Stainbank family in 1885 and today contains many of the original household contents which provide an interesting insight into colonial life. The castle is in the Kenneth Stainbank Nature Reserve, which protects an important remnant of the coastal forest that once covered much of the region.

A visit to the reserve shows what parts of Durban would have looked like 200 years ago. More than 300 species of bird and a relatively large number of mammals have been recorded here. Visitors can combine a visit to the castle with tea and a walk in the reserve. Many people pack a picnic to enjoy among the forest trees.

Coedmore Castle. Yellowwood Park.
Tel: (031) 469 8811.
www.yellowwoodpark.com.
Call to book a visit. Admission charge.
Kenneth Stainbank Nature Reserve.
Yellowwood Park. Tel: (031) 469 2807.
www.yellowwoodpark.com.
Open: 6am–6pm in summer;
6.30am–5.30pm in winter.
Small admission charge.

Durban City Hall, Durban Art Gallery and Natural Science Museum/Kwazuzukwazi Science Centre

The **City Hall** complex hosts civic functions and occasional symphony concerts. It also houses the **Durban Art Gallery** and **Natural Science Museum**. The Art Gallery has several important displays, including a comprehensive collection of Zulu beadwork, while the Natural Science Museum has good displays of animals and birds. Nearby, local history museums and the **Old House Museum** explain Durban's colonial history. The City Hall was built

in 1910, and is unusual in that it is a replica of the Belfast City Hall in Northern Ireland.

City Hall & Durban Art Gallery.
Dr Pixley Kaseme St.
Tel: (031) 311 2264. www.durban.gov.za.
Open: Mon–Sat 8.30am–5pm, Sun &
public holidays 11am–5pm.
Natural Science Museum.
Tel: (031) 311 2256. Same opening times
as City Hall.
Old House Museum.
31 Diakonia St. Tel: (031) 311 2261.
Open: Mon–Sat 8.30am–4pm, Sun &
public holidays 11am–4pm.

The Golden Mile

This 6km (3³/₄-mile) stretch of beaches has for decades been the focal point of holidaymakers seeking safe swimming, good surfing and entertainment at

Durban's City Hall is a replica of Belfast City Hall

night. Fun fairs, shallow paddling pools and innumerable restaurants help entertain those tired of the sun and sea.

Fringed by many high-rise hotels, the area is very busy during holidays and weekends. Visitors should be cautious of pickpockets and under no circumstances walk along back streets.

At the northern end of the Golden Mile is the **Fitzsimons Snake Park**, which houses South African reptiles. At the southern end of the 'Mile', uShaka Marine World has an excellent aquarium and dolphinarium (*see below*).

Fitzsimons Snake Park

240 O R Tambo Parade.
Tel: (031) 337 6465.
Open: daily 9.30am–4.30pm.
Demonstrations at regular intervals throughout the day.
Admission charge.

Durban's popular 'Golden Mile' beachfront

DIVING

The KwaZulu-Natal south coast has some excellent diving sites. On the Aliwal Shoal, divers are treated to regular sightings of ragged-tooth sharks, fearsome in appearance but docile in nature, moray eels and innumerable reef fish.

Large numbers of fish are also attracted to several wrecked ships, which act as artificial reefs. Further north, Umkomaas also offers good diving, and there are several other deeper sites suitable for experienced divers.

Contact **KwaZulu-Natal Tourism** for a comprehensive list of operators and dive sites. *Tel: (031) 366 7500. www.kzn.org.za*

uShaka Marine World

The aquarium and dolphinarium provide an exciting and comprehensive insight into the sea life of the warm waters of South Africa's east coast. Visitors can see sharks, turtles, dolphins and a wide variety of deep- and shallow-water fish, corals and seaweeds.

Displays include deep-water reefs and an interactive tidal pool where visitors are allowed to touch marine creatures and seaweeds. There is also a shipwreck reef. In this unique environment, visitors have the opportunity to snorkel with a huge variety of marine life.

There are freshwater displays focusing on the aquatic life encountered in KwaZulu-Natal's rivers and dams. Dolphin shows take place regularly, and water slides and a variety of other features provide entertainment for children.

1 Bell St. Tel: (031) 328 8000. www. ushakamarineworld.co.za. Open: Mon– Sun 9am–5pm. Admission charge.

Mosques and Hindu temples

Durban has a rich variety of Muslim mosques and Hindu temples, and several have been declared national monuments. The Juma Mosque is the largest Muslim place of worship in South Africa, and is a well-known landmark. Its golden domes and ornate architecture form the heart of a busy and colourful shopping area dominated by Indian-owned stores. There are several Hindu temples across the city and its outskirts, and the Alayam Hindu Temple provides an excellent example of temple architecture.

Contact KwaZulu-Natal Tourism for a comprehensive list of mosques and temples. Tel: (031) 366 7500. www.kzn.org.za

NSA Gallery

The NSA Gallery is situated among large old trees in Bulwer Park, and is divided into three exhibition areas, which provide a platform for the work of many young local artists. Exhibitions

Durban's Juma Mosque is South Africa's largest

change often, so it is best to check the latest programmes. There is also a gift shop and restaurant.

166 Bulwer Rd, Glenwood.
Tel: (031) 277 1705.
www.nsagallery.co.za.
Open: Tue–Fri 9am–5pm, Sat & Sun 10am–4pm. Closed: Mon.

Victoria Street Market

This market is housed indoors but is also surrounded by innumerable shops and pavement stalls that stretch for several city blocks.

A wide array of goods is available within the market and everyone expects to bargain. Spices, fabrics, Indian jewellery, Zulu beadwork, elaborately decorated spears, carved masks and even fresh fish are available. In a morning, visitors will meet an intriguing cross-section of Durban's residents.

Outside, street barbers offer quick haircuts to customers waiting for minibus taxis, while nearby vendors sell woven mats, clothing and live chickens.

Diving on the Aliwal Shoal, KwaZulu-Natal

Around Bertha Mkmise St and Denis Hurley St. Tel: (031) 306 4021.
Open: Mon–Sat 6am–5pm, Sun 10am–3pm.

Wilson's Wharf and The Point

Both these areas are close to the city centre and offer good harbour views. A variety of restaurants and pubs create a pleasant setting for lunchtime or evening meals. Wilson's Wharf overlooks a yacht marina and also has a good range of craft and curio shops. The Point is a great vantage point from which to watch vessels, ranging from small fishing boats to huge container ships, entering the busiest port in the country.
Wilson's Wharf. Boatman St.
The Point. Off Point Rd.
It is best to ask your hotel or tourist authorities for directions, and to arrange transport.

The long coastline offers fine angling opportunities

ANGLING

Both saltwater and freshwater angling enthusiasts will find ample opportunity to pursue their hobby in South Africa. Whether fishing from the beach for shad or grunter or from a boat for marlin and sailfish, anglers will be spoilt for choice. Saltwater fly-fishing is also widely followed, and the kingfish test even the best anglers.

Freshwater fly-fishing for trout has a large following, but recently the hard-fighting indigenous yellowfish is luring more and more anglers. Licences are required for all types of fishing but are easily acquired.

THE SOUTH COAST

The warm weather, laid-back attitude and good beaches make the South Coast a favourite holiday and retirement destination for many South Africans.

This region runs for 160km (100 miles) south of Durban and, in addition to its beaches, it has excellent seafood restaurants, markets, good golf courses and several crocodile farms, including the **Riverbend Crocodile Farm** on the Southern Explorer Route.

The **Oribi Gorge Nature Reserve** has about 35km (20 miles) of trails that wind in and out of a forested gorge, and fortunate visitors might spot some of the antelope and monkeys that live here.

The narrow-gauge **Banana Express** steam train runs from Port Shepstone to the Oribi Gorge Nature Reserve. The trip makes a good day trip, particularly for children.

*For Banana Express bookings, call
Port Shepstone Publicity.
Tel: (039) 682 2455. www.southcoast.
co.za. Call to confirm schedule.
Riverbend Crocodile Farm.
Tel: (039) 316 6204. www.crocodile
crazy.co.za. Open: daily 9am–4.30pm.*

THE NORTH COAST

The North Coast has been heavily
developed in recent years with a string
of upmarket hotels and holiday
developments running for some 50km
(30 miles) north of Durban.

It is a good place for an easily
arranged stress-free holiday with plenty
of safe swimming beaches, good
restaurants and other entertainment.
Dolphins are often spotted along this
coast, hence its popular name of the
Dolphin Coast.
*Dolphin Coast Publicity Association.
Tel: (032) 946 1256. www.dolphin
coast.kzn.org.za*

Natal Sharks Board

Sharks are widely feared, but most
people's terror is based on
misconceptions. The Board offers
comprehensive audiovisual displays and
lectures, dispelling some of the myths
about these creatures which fill an
important ecological niche. Sharks
caught in the shark nets that protect
many beaches are sometimes dissected
during tours.

The Board is situated at Umhlanga
Rocks some 20km (12 miles) north of
Durban. They monitor the shark nets

A Zulu man in traditional dress at Shakaland

that protect many of KwaZulu-Natal's
bathing beaches, and boat tours can
be arranged.
*Tel: (031) 566 0400. www.shark.co.za.
Exhibition & shop open: Mon–Fri
8am–4pm. Audiovisual presentation &
shark dissection: Tue–Thur 9am & 2pm,
Sun 2pm. Admission charge.*

Shakaland

Shakaland offers an 'interactive'
experience of life in a Zulu *kraal*
(settlement) a hundred years ago. Zulu
warriors with shields and spears dance
for guests, storytellers recount tales of
kings and queens, and guides explain
local traditions. Overnight
accommodation is provided in 'beehive
huts' made of grass woven over wooden
poles. Traditional food, including the
staple *phutu* (a stiff porridge made
from de-husked maize) and indigenous
(*Cont. on p126*)

Game reserves of Zululand and Maputaland

The spectacular game reserves of Zululand offer protection to a bewildering array of animals, birds, fish and plant life, and help make the region one of South Africa's top wildlife areas.

These reserves are some of the oldest in Africa. The Hluhluwe Imfolozi Park was created as two separate parks in 1896, and has been the core of more than 100 years of pioneering conservation work, including the epic effort that saved the white rhino from extinction.

In the Greater St Lucia Wetlands Park, elephants and black rhinos browse within sight of hippos and crocodiles. A few kilometres away, the warm Indian Ocean nurtures coral reefs and prolific sea life, including humpback whales passing by on their annual migration.

Lake St Lucia, which is really an estuary and one of the largest lakes in Africa, is surrounded by varying forms of forest, grasslands and woodlands. In addition to the elephants and rhinos, these areas support buffalo, leopard, zebra, reedbuck and many other species of mammal, as well as prolific birdlife.

High, forested sand dunes, among the highest in the world, roll down

See leatherback turtles on the beaches of Greater St Lucia Wetlands Park

The Greater St Lucia Wetlands Park has a large crocodile population

right to the edge of wide, sandy beaches. In summer, the beaches are used as nesting sites by loggerhead turtles and huge leatherback turtles (really big specimens can weigh up to 600kg/1,320lb). The turtles lay their eggs towards the end of the year. Just over two months later, the babies make their first foray into the sea. Authorities run strictly controlled tours to watch both the nesting and hatching processes.

Various coral reefs fringe the shoreline, providing excellent snorkelling and diving.

There are several other parks along the coast, including Kosi Bay and Mapelane. Kosi Bay is one of the most important estuary systems in the country, and acts as a nursery for marine fish. There are also coral reefs at the mouth of the system, which consists of four lakes of increasing salinity.

Further inland, neighbouring Mkhuze Game Reserve and the Phongola Biosphere Reserve offer protection to a wide range of species and their habitat.

Not far away is Hluhluwe Imfolozi Park, where conservationists managed to save the white rhino from possible extinction. These large, docile creatures had been hunted mercilessly until the 1920s, by which time their numbers had dwindled to a few dozen.

A few far-sighted conservationists pressed for a special programme to protect the white rhino, and also the black, and today South Africa is the stronghold of the world population. Worldwide, some 11,000 white rhinos live in the wild and in zoos, but only about 3,300 black rhinos exist.

The area between the Black Umfolozi and White Umfolozi rivers was once the hunting ground of the Zulu King Shaka, and was off limits to commoners and outsiders. This restriction helped maintain the wildlife population before the first white settlers arrived.

Other protected areas include the mountainous Ithala Game Reserve and the Ndumo Game Reserve, which are two of the country's top birding spots with more than 400 species having been recorded. There are many privately run game reserves and lodges throughout the region, which also offer excellent accommodation and good game viewing.
Tel: (033) 845 1000.
www.kznwildlife.com

vegetables are also available but not compulsory.

Shakaland is some 162km (100 miles) north of Durban near the town of Eshowe. Tel: (035) 460 0912. www.shakaland.com to arrange visits and book accommodation.

Opens at 11am.

Admission charge.

RESERVES AND PARKS
Greater St Lucia Wetlands Park

This World Heritage Site is actually an amalgamation of several reserves. It encompasses a wide range of habitats, including the huge Lake St Lucia, beaches, coral reefs, grasslands and woodlands. Elephants, rhino, buffalo and antelope occur on the shores of the lake, and the reefs offer excellent diving and snorkelling. Birdlife is exceptional. The beaches are broad and clean, and the water is warm nearly all year round.

Accommodation ranges from comfortable lodges to camping, and many companies arrange tours. Sodwana Bay provides the easiest access points to the best coral reefs. There are self-catering chalets and privately run lodges and other accommodation nearby.

Hluhluwe Imfolozi Park

There is no easier place in the world to see rhinos in the wild. Around 1,200 white and 300 black rhino live in the park, which constitutes one-tenth of the global population, and that's including animals in captivity.

All the other members of the 'Big Five' live here, as well as large populations of giraffe, nyala and other species. The Mpila and Hilltop camps offer accommodation ranging from self-catering in safari tents to upmarket, fully serviced lodges. There are also several 'bush lodges' which are set away from the main camps.

Short walks with skilled guides can be arranged and should not be missed. Longer three- and four-day trails, where walkers camp in the bush, are also on offer. Night drives can be booked and are another 'must do', as they enable visitors to see many nocturnal species that might otherwise be missed.

Ithala Game Reserve

Although less well known than some of the other parks, Ithala nevertheless is well worth visiting for its variety of habitat alone. The landscape is extremely rugged, and high mountains drop steeply down to the hot valley of the Pongola River.

Elephant, rhino and buffalo are regularly spotted, and the reserve is an excellent place to see the nocturnal aardwolf, which, although it is as big as a medium-sized dog, lives on ants. The award-winning Ntshondwe Camp is built on the side of the Ngotshe mountains.

Ndumo and Mkuse Game Reserves

Both these reserves offer excellent game viewing and are two of South Africa's premier birding sites. Ndumo is located on the border of Mozambique, and its many pans (small natural lakes), fringed with the yellow-barked fever trees, create a sense of tropical Africa. Thick forest and dense reed beds add to the atmosphere of adventure.

Although neither reserve is very large, they are both enormously diverse. *Ndumo and Mkuse Game Reserves. Tel: (027) 86010 19008 (toll free). Ezemvelo KZN Wildlife. Tel: (033) 845 1000. www. kznwildlife.com. Contact KZN Tourism for a comprehensive list of private reserves and lodges. Tel: (027) 87803 4636 (toll free). www.kzn.org.za. Parks open all year round.*

The uKhahlamba Drakensberg Park

This 250,000-hectare (620,000-acre) Park is also a World Heritage Site, and throughout the mountain range sheer cliffs, steep, sandstone-fringed foothills and cold, clear streams create a peaceful world far removed from the hustle and bustle of cities.

Summers are warm with regular thunderstorms. Winters can be icy with occasional snowfalls, and many high-altitude streams freeze at night. Peaks here average over 3,000m (9,840ft).

The entire range offers excellent hiking, horse riding and birding. Large game is scarce at high altitude but many small species do occur. The rare bearded vulture is often seen, as are

Champagne Castle, uKhahlamba Drakensberg Mountains

black eagles, lanner falcons and a host of smaller birds.

These mountains proved to be one of the last refuges of the San (Bushmen). Hundreds of their rock paintings and engravings can be found in the caves and rock shelters of the foothills known as the 'Little Berg'.

There are plenty of hotels, B&Bs and guest farms dotted along the entire length of the mountain range, and these offer a wide range of activities, including tennis, fly-fishing, mountain-bike riding, abseiling and other sports. The park comprises many smaller reserves, including those listed below.

Didima Camp (Cathedral Peak)

Didima offers the best of both worlds – the outdoor splendour of the mountains and the luxurious comfort of imaginatively designed chalets and a restaurant.

There is a comprehensive San art interpretive centre where the long, and sometimes sad, history of the San is explained. The display also explains the spiritual role art played in the life of these nomadic hunters.

For the fit, there are day hikes to the top of Cathedral Peak. Many easier walks are, however, accessible, and if the going gets too hot, a plunge into a mountain pool is likely to invigorate even the most weary of hikers.

Giant's Castle

Set above the clear Bushman's River, the main rest camp has spectacular views of the high, blue-grey walls and peaks of the uKhahlamba Drakensberg (*uKhahlamba* means 'barrier of spears' in Zulu and *Drakensberg* means 'dragon mountain' in Afrikaans).

The San once hunted eland and other animals in the deep valleys beneath 'the Giant'. Hundreds of

No need to worry – the Cannibal Cave hiking trail is great fun

The rolling sugar-cane fields and plantations of the KwaZulu-Natal Midlands

their rock paintings and engravings can be found in the many caves and rock shelters in the area. One of the best collections is at the main caves just a short walk from the comfortable main camp.

Visitors spend time hiking, horse riding, trout fishing or simply relaxing at the edge of a mountain stream or in the quiet gardens of the rest camp itself. Injisuthi camp, further north, offers self-catering chalets and tents in a remote valley surrounded by sandstone cliffs.

Royal Natal and Rugged Glen

The breathtaking 5km (3-mile)-long sheer wall of the Amphitheatre is the focal point of Royal Natal. The Thukela River starts life high on the summit before tumbling down sheer cliffs to form one of the highest waterfalls in the world.

Royal Natal offers the tranquillity found throughout the 'Berg' and is one of South Africa's most popular mountain destinations. Hikes and rides ranging from a few hours to several days can be undertaken along well-marked paths, and trout fishing and horse riding are also very popular.

Elsewhere in the Berg

There are other provincial parks including the Coleford, Kamberg and Loteni nature reserves, as well as dozens of private hotels, guest farms and B&Bs.

The Giant's Cup and Mkhomazi Wilderness Areas offer exhilarating hiking along the face of the mountains, with overnight stops in caves or mountain huts. These hikes are for the fit only, but well worth the time and effort.

Parks open all year round.
Contact Ezemvelo KZN Wildlife.
Tel: (033) 845 1000.
www.kznwildlife.com.
Contact KZN Tourism for a list of
private lodges, B&Bs, campsites
and tours.
Tel: (027) 87803 4636 (toll free).
www.kzn.org.za

THE MIDLANDS

Set among the lush green hills, the
Midlands Meander arts and craft route
runs through some of KwaZulu-Natal's
most beautiful scenery. More than 160
craft shops, art galleries, restaurants,
hotels and B&Bs are scattered along
country roads beginning about 25km
(15 miles) north of Pietermaritzburg.

The area is ideal for weekends spent
wandering around, while shopping and
stopping for lunch, dinner or a cup of
tea. Just outside the town of Howick,
the Umgeni River tumbles over the
95m (312ft)-high Howick Falls.
At nearby Midmar Dam and the
surrounding nature reserve, there is an
historical village and open-air museum.
The area offers good watersports, horse
riding and game viewing.

It is best to visit the Meander website
or to get a copy of their extensive
brochure to plan your trip according
to your tastes.
Midlands Meander Association.
Tel: (023) 330 8195.
www.midlandsmeander.co.za

PIETERMARITZBURG

This sleepy city is the capital of the
province, and was established by the
Boer Voorterkkers fleeing British rule

The Valley of a Thousand Hills near Durban

in 1838. The British took over the city in 1843, and it became the capital of the Colony of Natal. The city still has many buildings dating from the 19th century, including the all-brick town hall, the Old Natal Parliament and the railway station. Seventy of these buildings are national monuments, and self-guided trails enable visitors to see many of them in a few hours' walk.

The **Voortrekker/Msunduzi Museum**, housed in the small gabled Church of the Vow, was erected in 1841 by the Boers. It commemorates the Battle of Blood River, and depicts life during that time. The nearby **Natal Museum** is devoted to the region's social and natural history. The **Tatham Art Gallery** contains European and South African works, and there are also a number of interesting churches, mosques and Hindu temples in the city. *Pieteramaritzburg Tourism.*
177 Commercial Rd. Tel: (033) 345 1348.
www.pmbtourism.co.za

Handmade carpets for sale in the Midlands

Voortrekker/Msunduzi Museum.
351 Longmarket St.
Tel: (033) 394 6834.
Open: Mon–Fri 9am–4pm, Sat 9am–1pm.
Natal Museum.
237 Jabu Ndlova St.
Tel: (033) 345 1404. www.nmsa.org.za.
Open: Mon–Fri 8.15am–4.30pm, Sat 9am–4pm, Sun 10am–3pm.
Tatham Art Gallery.
Tel: (033) 392 2800.
www.tatham.org.za.
Open: Mon–Fri 8am–5pm.

GANDHI

Pietermaritzburg played an ungracious but important role in the early life of Indian pacifist Mohandas Gandhi (later known as Mahatma). In 1893, he was evicted from the first-class carriage of a train at Pietermaritzburg Station because of his race. He later said the incident triggered his philosophy of passive resistance based on truth and compassion.

Gandhi became an international symbol of passive resistance, and a statue in his memory was erected outside the Old Colonial Building in 1993.

Tour: KwaZulu-Natal battlefields

Some of the fiercest battles ever fought in South Africa raged across the hills and valleys of KwaZulu-Natal throughout the 19th century.

Allow two days. Start at Spioenkop, which is about 150km (94 miles) north of Pietermaritzburg on the N3 freeway. At the N11 junction, turn left to Spioenkop, which is about 18km (12 miles) west of the freeway.

Early Boer settlers clashed several times with Zulu armies in the late 1830s. In 1879, the ferocious Anglo-Zulu War brought the eventual destruction of the Zulu Army. During the South African War (Second Boer War) of 1899–1902, some of the worst fighting took place in KwaZulu-Natal. Dozens of other battles also took place.

www.battlefields.kzn.org.za

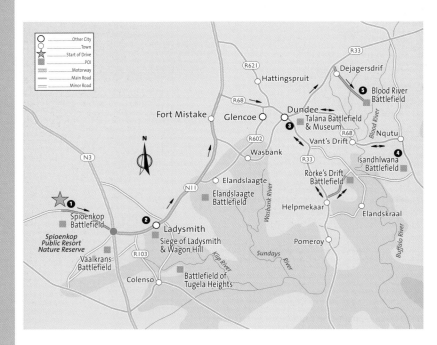

British graves at the Talana Battlefield, KwaZulu-Natal

Isandhlwana, the site of a famous Zulu victory over the British

1 Spioenkop

Earlier British forces sent to relieve Ladysmith fought a bitter battle against the Boers for the strategic mountain of Spioenkop which overlooks Ladysmith.
Spioenkop walk and tape tours available. Tel: (036) 448 1557. www.drakensberg-tourism.com. Open: daily 6am–6pm.

Retrace your route to the N3, and Ladysmith is a further 14km (9 miles) to the east along the N11.

2 Siege of Ladysmith

In one of the most famous battles of the South African War, Boer commandos surrounded British forces in Ladysmith and kept them trapped there for 118 days. The water supply ran out, food shortages became acute and disease broke out, killing many in the town. Both defenders and attackers took heavy casualties in the fighting

until the town was relieved on 28 February 1900.
Ladysmith Siege Museum. Tel: (036) 637 2992. Open: Mon–Fri 9am–4pm, Sat 9am–1pm.

From Ladysmith, take the N11 north for about 75km (47 miles) until the junction with the R68 to Dundee.

Follow the R68 for 22km (13 miles). Talana Battlefield is on the eastern side of the town.

3 Talana Battlefield

This was the scene of the first battle between the British and the Boers in 1899. The Boers won the battle, and the British retreated to Ladysmith where they were later trapped. Graves and monuments mark the site of the battle. There is also a **museum** that documents Dundee's history as a coal-mining and glass-manufacturing town.
Talana Museum. Tel: (034) 212 2654. www.talana.co.za. Open: Mon–Fri

8am–4.30pm, Sat & Sun 9am–4.30pm.
Choice of guided or self-guided tours
of battlefield.
Tour Dundee.
Tel: (034) 218 2837.
www.tourdundee.co.za. Open: Mon–Fri
8am–4.30pm, Sat, Sun & public holidays
10am–4pm. Closed: Christmas Day.

It is about 45km (28 miles) from Dundee
to Rorke's Drift on the R68. Follow the
signs to Isandhlwana, which is about
30km (18 miles) further.

4 Isandhlwana and Rorke's Drift

On 22 January 1879, the Zulu Army,
although later vanquished, inflicted the
largest ever defeat on the British
colonial army at Isandhlwana. More
than 870 British soldiers were killed.

Several Zulu regiments then moved
on to attack Rorke's Drift where a small
number of men fought vastly superior
forces for more than 12 hours. Eleven
of the defenders later received the

The Rorke's Drift Museum, KwaZulu-Natal

Victoria Cross, Britain's highest award
for bravery.

There is a good arts and crafts centre
over the road from the **museum**.
Isandhlwana Battle site enquiries:
tel: (034) 271 8165. Open: Mon–Fri
8am–6pm, Sat & Sun 9am–4pm.
Rorke's Drift Museum.
Tel: (034) 642 1687.
Open: daily 8am–4pm.

From Rorke's Drift, follow the road back
to the R68, and then head towards
Dundee. Take the R33 going northeast of
Dundee. Turn off to Blood River after
27km (16 miles), and the battlefield is a
further 20km (12 miles) southeast.

5 Blood River Battlefield

This battle forms one of the cornerstones
of Afrikaner history. The battle was the
result of an attempt to punish the Zulus
for what the Voortrekkers believed to be
the murder of one of their leaders. A
small Voortrekker party took on a far
superior Zulu force and won. There is a
replica *laager* (circle) of 68 wagons
commemorating the Boer victory, and
also a monument to the Zulu soldiers
who died.

Today, the 1838 battlefield is a
hallowed spot for some Afrikaners
who believe that their God supported
them in defeating the Zulus.
Ncome Museum.
Tel: (034) 271 8121.
www.ncomemuseum.co.za.
Open: Mon–Sun 9am–4pm.
Free admission.

Tour: Old Zulu Kingdom

Old Zululand covered a vast tract of central KwaZulu-Natal. One of the most interesting sections lies north of Durban, particularly between the Tugela River and the Swazi border. Here, there are Zulu homesteads, historic battlegrounds, memorials and forts.

Allow at least two days. Start at Stanger and drive up the N2 for 56km (35 miles) to Gingindlovu.

1 Gingindlovu

Gingindlovu (meaning 'swallower of the elephant') was the site of a military *kraal* (settlement) built by Cetshwayo (Zulu chief Shaka's nephew) to commemorate victory over his brother, Mbulazi, in their contest for the Zulu throne.
From Gingindlovu, take the R66 to Eshowe (26km/16 miles).

2 Eshowe

Eshowe ('sound of wind in the trees') was a quiet summer retreat for the Zulus. Cetshwayo's first *kraal* was here in 1860, before he moved to Ulundi. It was

Traditional Zulu crafts

replaced by the British-built **Fort Nongqayi** (1883), now the Zululand Historical Museum. Near Nkandla Forest Reserve ('place of exhaustion') is the grave of Cetshwayo, who died in 1884.
Fort Nongqayi. Nongqayi Rd. Tel: (035) 474 2281. Open: Mon–Sat 9am–4pm.

For Shaka's Kraal, take the R68 north from Eshowe (6km/4 miles), and then right on the R230 (dirt road) for about 20km (12 miles).
  Continue along the R68 to Melmoth (27km/17 miles), then turn on to the R34 and continue for 24km (15 miles) to uMgungundlovu.

3 uMgungundlovu

King Dingane moved the Zulu capital to uMgungundlovu ('place of the great elephant'), where Voortrekker leader Piet Retief and his men were executed in February 1838. Retribution was grim: 3,000 warriors were killed at the Battle of Blood River (*see p135*). The uMgungundlovu Museum occupies the

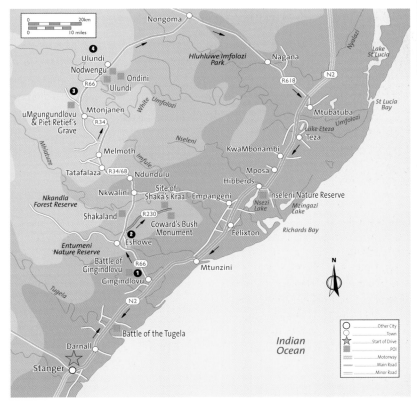

site of the *kraal*, the core of which has been accurately rebuilt.
Take the R66 to Ulundi (about 18km/ 11 miles).

4 Ulundi

Ulundi was Cetshwayo's capital (1873). The British destroyed it in 1879, finally breaking Zulu military power. A second capital at Ondini ('the heights') was burnt by the Swazis. The local government rebuilt it as the **KwaZulu Cultural Museum**, and the royal quarters have been re-created. Close to

Ulundi is the eMakhosini Valley and royal burial ground. From Ulundi, the route continues east, passing through the Hluhluwe Imfolozi Park (*see p126*).
KwaZulu Cultural Museum.
3km (2 miles) east of town at Ondini. Tel: (035) 870 2052. www.heritagekzn. co.za. Open: Mon–Fri 8am–4pm, Sat & Sun 9am–4pm.
Admission charge for both museums.

Leave the park on the R618 road and, at the junction with the N2, head south and back via Stanger to Durban.

Lesotho and Swaziland

Although these tiny nations are both independent, their tourism industries are closely linked to South Africa. Both countries are poor and predominantly rural. Swaziland has a pleasant climate, although parts can be hot in summer, and Lesotho, home to the indigenous Basotho people, is very mountainous and cold in winter. Swaziland has several good hiking trails and game reserves, while Lesotho is famous for pony trekking.

Lesotho

The high Maluti and Drakensberg mountains dominate most of this tiny kingdom's scenery. Life among the rugged mountains is harsh, and heavy snowfalls with temperatures way below freezing are common in winter. Many of the mountain peaks are higher than 2,500m (8,200ft), and no point in the country is less than 1,000m (3,300ft)

A Basotho man with his traditional hat and blanket

above sea level. There are several places where beautiful San rock art can be viewed, Iron Age depictions of elands, cattle and hunters. Adventurous travellers can scour Lesotho's ancient rocks for the many fossilised dinosaur footprints.

Several companies run pony-trekking operations and guided hikes. Trips in 4WDs across the mountains are also available. The horse, or more specifically the Basotho pony (a small, stocky, shaggy-coated horse), is the primary source of transport for many people in the mountains. Although crops are grown at lower levels, most people living at high altitude depend on sheep, goat and, to a lesser degree, cattle herding for a living. Lesotho is entirely surrounded by South Africa, and most of its citizens earn their livelihoods there. The capital city of Maseru has some interesting craft shops, but the real beauty of the country lies in the mountains, waterfalls and deep valleys. *www.seelesotho.com*

Swaziland

This small, predominantly rural, kingdom is sandwiched between South Africa's eastern border and Mozambique. Many Swazis have relatives living in South Africa on whom they are economically dependent. Even so, Swaziland has a distinct cultural identity that sets it apart from its much larger neighbour, with interesting royal traditions. The Milwane Game Reserve, set in the fertile Ezulweni Valley, offers good game-viewing and horse riding, and the country's nicest guesthouses can be found in this area. Further north, the hills of the Malalotja Nature Reserve are an excellent hiking destination. The Ezulweni Valley has several hotels, golf courses, and craft and art shops.

Swazi crafts on sale near Mbabane

The capital, Mbabane, is 360km (224 miles) from Johannesburg by road. The main border is open from 6am–9pm, though driving to Swaziland via Barberton and Pigg's Peak is the most scenic route.
www.welcometoswaziland.com

Lesotho and Swaziland

Swazi women in traditional dress

Shopping

South Africa has a huge variety of goods to tempt both the casual souvenir-hunters and serious shoppers. Prices vary: shopping malls and high streets, particularly those in tourist areas, tend to be the most expensive, market stalls less so and roadside vendors the cheapest. However, quality does vary and shoppers should be cautious when buying at the roadside. Market traders and roadside vendors expect to bargain, but shop owners in upmarket malls are less flexible and seldom oblige with lower prices.

ANTIQUES

Antiques have risen in price in recent years, but many dealers sell quality products that may tempt collectors of Africana and knowledgeable buyers.

For a list of the shops, phone the **South African Antique Dealers' Association**. *Tel: (011) 880 0815. www.saada.co.za*

West African masks for sale at the Rosebank African Craft Market

Colourful curio shops on the Garden Route

BOOKS AND MAPS

Exclusive Books and **CNA** stores have branches throughout the country.
www.exclusivebooks.com; www.cna.co.za

Cape Town
Clarke's Bookshop

Rare and second-hand books, prints and maps, as well as books on South Africa.
211 Long St. Tel: (021) 423 5739.
www.clarkesbooks.co.za

Durban
Adams & Co

Long-established bookshop selling general and children's books, and a large range of academic texts.

341 West St. Tel: (086) 134 1341.
www.adamsbooks.co.za

Johannesburg
Exclusive Books

Flagship store of a large chain with more than 50 outlets all over South Africa, stocking fiction and non-fiction books of all kinds.
50 Bath Ave, The Mall of Rosebank.
Tel: (011) 447 3028.

CURIOS, ARTS AND CRAFTS

A wide range of wooden masks, carved animals, wooden headrests, beadwork and weaving from all over Africa are sold at markets

The Addy Hoyle art gallery, Clarens

and by roadside vendors. The quality of some of these products is extremely good, and knowledgeable buyers should be able to make reasonable buys.

Many of these products are sold by migrants from elsewhere in Africa, and chatting with them about their travels can be an interesting experience. Some people take weeks to get to South Africa, travelling by bus or lorry with their goods.

Be cautious when buying pottery, carvings and other wooden products at the roadside or at markets. Examine the carvings for cracks that are sometimes disguised with wood filler or shoe polish. Try to establish whether pottery or ceramic items have been properly fired, especially when shopping in rural areas.

Cape Town
Heartworks
South African ceramics, beadwork and other items for the home.
98 Kloof St. Tel: (021) 424 8419.

Clarens
Addy Hoyle
Art gallery containing mainly local paintings of landscapes and animals.
Clarens, Free State.
Tel: (058) 256 1875.
www.addyhoyle.co.za

Durban
Africa Art Gallery
Painting, sculptures and other works by some of South Africa's best artists.
7 Chartwell Centre, Umhlanga Rocks.
Tel: (031) 561 2661.
www.africaartgallery.co.za

Johannesburg
Art Africa
Ethnic arts and collectables from many parts of sub-Saharan Africa.
62 Tyrone Ave, Parkview.
Tel: (011) 486 2052.

Kim Sacks Gallery and School of Ceramics
Selection of art, jewellery and ceramics.
153 Jan Smuts Ave, Parkwood.
Tel: (011) 447 5804.

KwaZulu-Natal Midlands
Kingdom Weavers
African rugs, tapestries and other items.
Curry's Post, Balgowan.
Tel: (033) 234 4205.

GEMSTONES AND JEWELLERY
Many South African dealers sell top-quality gems and jewellery, and tourists benefit from a VAT (14 per cent) rebate on leaving the country. The jeweller will assist you with the paperwork. This rebate only applies in shops accredited by the Jewellery Council of South Africa.
Jewellery Council of South Africa
Tel: (011) 554 7958.
www.jewellerysa.com

Cape Town
Olga Jewellery Design Studio
Skilfully created jewellery of all types, including unique diamond pieces, which can be tailored to personal preferences by one of South Africa's leading designers.

Victoria Wharf. Tel: (021) 419 8016.
www.olgajewellers.co.za

Johannesburg
Charles Grieg
100-year-old family business at the forefront of South African jewellery.
Shop U25, Sandton City.
Tel: (011) 783 2714.

MARKETS
Many cities, towns and villages hold markets at weekends. Check with local tourist authorities for locations and times.

Cape Town
Green Point Fleamarket
Everything and anything from art and clothes to cheese and *biltong*.

Street musicians entertain shoppers

Green Point Stadium. Open: Sun & some public holidays, weather permitting.

Durban
Amphitheatre Market
Fleamarket with over 700 stalls.
North Beach. Open: last Sun of each month.

Fine dining in The Mall of Rosebank

Johannesburg
Newtown Market Africa
Cosmopolitan Saturday hub. Antique African costume, masks, junk and beads.
Newtown Cultural Precinct. Open: Sat 9am–4pm.

OUTDOOR EQUIPMENT
Cape Town
Cape Union Mart
Gear for camping, climbing and hiking.
Victoria Wharf, The Waterfront.
Tel: 0860 034 000 (toll free).
Branches nationwide.

Surf Centre
Beach and casual clothing, wetsuits and the like. Primarily women's wear, but also has men's section.
454 Canal Walk Centre, Century City, Milnerton.
Tel: (021) 555 4970.

Johannesburg
Cape Union Mart
Everything for the outdoors from penknives to sleeping bags.
Hyde Park Shopping Mall.
Tel: 0860 034 000.
Branches nationwide.

Outdoor Warehouse
Tents, camping, hiking equipment and everything for outdoor pursuits.
8 Tungsten St, Strijdom Park, Randburg.
Tel: (011) 792 8331.
Several branches nationwide.

SHOPPING MALLS
Cape Town
Cavendish Square
Award-winning complex with over 200 shops, and several cinemas and restaurants.
Vineyard Rd, Claremont.
Tel: (021) 657 5620.
www.cavendish.co.za

Durban
Gateway Theatre of Shopping
Shopping, leisure and entertainment under one roof. Also extreme sports facilities.
Durban North. Tel: (031) 514 0500.
www.gatewayworld.co.za

Johannesburg
The Mall of Rosebank
Fashionable shopping, cinemas, restaurants and fleamarkets on Sundays. The Zone opposite the mall connects to the new Gautrain Rapid Rail Link (*www.gautrain.co.za*).
Tel: (011) 788 5530.
www.themallofrosebank.co.za

Pretoria
Menlyn Park Shopping Centre
Same attractions as most other centres, but with a rooftop drive-in cinema.
Menlyn, Pretoria.
Tel: (012) 471 0600.
www.menlynpark.co.za

WILD ANIMAL PRODUCTS
Various wild animal products, including trophies, skins, leather belts

Part of the Spier Wine Cellar range

and shoes, are sold at markets and in shops. Whatever one's view on buying these products, it should be remembered that many countries have strict rules concerning the importation of animal products. It is also illegal to sell ivory and some other animal products, including the skin of the African rock python.

Should you be offered ivory or any other animal product you suspect to be illegal, it is best to notify the police or conservation authorities. Youngsters at the side of the road commonly sell tortoises, but this trade is illegal and should be reported.

WINE
Nearly all cellars are willing to ship wine overseas. Local wines are usually a good buy in comparison with international prices. Wine dealers will also be able to advise on customs limitations on quantities that may be imported to various countries.

Entertainment

Entertainment in South Africa is eclectic and mirrors the broad range of cultures and traditions of the country's people. Music and theatre often take on cross-cultural flavours, although Shakespeare and more traditionally Western plays are firm favourites in some circles. The government has taken to heart the development of the performing arts, and the Department of Arts, Culture, Science and Technology is active in the promotion of theatre, music and other disciplines throughout the country.

LISTINGS

Check local daily newspapers for listings sections. The national *Mail&Guardian* newspaper, published every Friday, gives excellent coverage to major cities. The *Mail&Guardian* also has a very good entertainment section on its website: *www.mg.co.za*

Most regional tourism websites have links to what's on in their areas.

BOOKING TICKETS

Many theatre, opera, ballet, sports match and concert tickets can be bought through Computicket, which has outlets in every Shoprite and Checkers supermarket nationwide.

Open: Mon–Fri 9am–5pm, Sat 9am–4pm. Cash or credit card.

They also handle online and telephone bookings.

Nationwide call centre.

Tel: (083) 915 8000.

www.computicket.com

BALLET AND DANCE

Traditional ballets are regularly performed in the larger centres, but less commonly so in smaller towns and rural areas. Highly talented local dancers perform in most productions, and an increasing number of international companies and dancers are visiting South Africa.

Dance takes on many forms in South Africa, and ranges from traditional Zulu and Venda dances that have been performed for centuries to various forms of modern dance, tap and classical. The best traditional dancing is often performed at cultural villages in rural parts of the country where cultural links to the past are usually stronger than those in the cosmopolitan cities. At many of these performances the performers will explain the significance of each dance and what role it plays in society. Some dances are performed only at weddings, others are linked to seasonal festivals and some are just for fun.

Traditional dance is also often incorporated into music performances with band members and vocalists joining in. Ballroom dancing is extremely popular, particularly in townships. Children and adults get togged up in formal suits and dresses and compete for national awards.

THEATRE

As with music, theatre in South Africa reflects the diversity of the population. A Chekhov play may be running at one theatre while a John Kani production is on at the next, and some other theatre work that falls into no particular camp will also attract audiences.

Much of South Africa's modern theatre has drawn on the experiences of the political struggle, although many playwrights are now exploring new themes. Cultural officers work throughout the country to encourage youngsters, and to assist existing groups to develop and improve their skills in the performing arts.

Cape Town
Artscape Theatre Centre
Theatre, ballet, opera, classical music.
DF Malan St, Foreshore.
Tel: (021) 410 9800.
www.artscape.co.za
The Baxter Theatre Centre
A Cape Town institution. Theatre, ballet and classical music.
Main Rd, Rondebosch.
Tel: (021) 685 7880.
www.baxter.co.za

The Playhouse Theatre, Durban

Independent Armchair Theatre
Hosts an unusual array of comedy and other entertainment, often by young performers.
135 Main Rd, Observatory.
Tel: (021) 447 1514.
www.myspace.com/armchairtheatre

Darling
Evita se Perron
Hilarious shows by Pieter-Dirk Uys, South Africa's foremost satirist.
Darling Station, Arcadia Rd. (Darling is about an hour's drive north of Cape Town.)

Cape Town City Hall

Tel: (022) 492 3930.
www.evita.co.za

Durban
The Playhouse Theatre
A Durban favourite. Theatre, classical music and other shows performed in three venues.
Smith St, opposite City Hall.
Tel: (031) 369 9555.
www.playhousecompany.com

Johannesburg
Joburg Theatre
Comprises three theatres: large, middle-sized and small.
Loveday St, Braamfontein.
Tel: (011) 877 6800.
www.joburgtheatre.com

Liberty Theatre on the Square
Small, comfortable theatre.
Nelson Mandela Sq, Sandton.
Tel: (011) 883 8606.

The Market Theatre
A theatre with a proud history of hosting politically sensitive plays and supporting black actors.
Newtown Precinct. Tel: (011) 832 1641.
www.markettheatre.co.za

Pretoria
South African State Theatre
Theatre, classical music and opera in several venues.
320 Pretoria St.
Tel: (012) 392 4000.
www.statetheatre.co.za

CINEMA

The South African film industry is developing in leaps and bounds, and many international studios are using South Africa as a filming location. Most large centres hold regular film festivals, details of which are usually listed in local newspapers and on tourism authority websites.

Ster-Kinekor and Nu Metro, the two largest distributors of films in South Africa, have screens all over the country, mostly in shopping malls. Local newspapers publish film listings. Some cinemas are not part of the major commercial networks and often show films not distributed on circuit.

Drive-in cinemas can still be found in some areas.

Nu Metro
Tel: (086) 124 6362. www.numetro.co.za
Ster-Kinekor
Tel: (082) 16789. www.sterkinekor.com

Cape Town
The Iziko-SA National Gallery
Sometimes shows documentaries and films by local independent film-makers. Check their listings sheets.
Government Ave.
Tel: (021) 456 1628.

The Labia
A favourite Cape Town venue. Fashionably laid-back, with a bar downstairs.
68 Orange St, Gardens.
Tel: (021) 424 5927. www.labia.co.za

Johannesburg
Cinema Nouveau
Shows a variety of limited release and alternative films.
The Mall of Rosebank. Tel: (082) 16789.

MUSIC

Whatever your taste in music you should be able to find it in South Africa, and there might even be something completely new. South African music is increasingly influenced by the music of Africa, particularly West and Central Africa, and any number of bands and performers can be found experimenting with new trends.

Jazz, blues and reggae are hugely popular among the majority of the population. The younger generation favour *kwaito* (the South African form of rap), trance, house and general pop. There are also a variety of venues that play good old-fashioned rock and roll. Check the local paper to see what's on. Occasionally rock concerts featuring international and local stars are hosted at sports stadiums or indoor arenas.

Opera and classical music are often performed in the larger cities, sometimes in the grand old buildings built as town halls. Theatre and opera-goers usually dress fairly smartly but leave their best clothes for opening nights.

Cape Town
Cape Town City Hall
Home of the Cape Philharmonic Orchestra, which produces classical music in grand surroundings.

Darling St. Tel: (021) 410 9809.
www.cpo.org.za

Green Dolphin
Live jazz and dining.
V&A Waterfront. Tel: (021) 421 7471.
Open: daily.

Durban
Catalina Theatre
Operettas, classical music.
Wilsons Wharf. Tel: (031) 305 6889.
www.catalinatheatre.co.za

Durban City Hall
Home of the KZN Philharmonic
Orchestra. Classical music and other
concerts.

Smith St. Tel: (031) 369 9438.
www.kznpo.co.za

Johannesburg
Linder Auditorium
Home base of the Johannesburg
Philharmonic Orchestra (JPO).
Wits Education Campus,
St Andrews Rd, Parktown.
Tel: (011) 789 2733.
Bookings through Computicket.

OPEN-AIR VENUES
Cape Town
Kirstenbosch Summer Sunset
Hosts jazz, classical music and
choral concerts. In winter, the visitor
centre hosts concerts.

A summer evening concert at the Kirstenbosch National Botanical Garden

Kirstenbosch National Botanical Garden, Rhodes Dr, Newlands. Tel: (021) 799 8899. www.sanbi.org

Oude Libertas Amphitheatre
Classical music and dance.
Adam Tas Rd, Stellenbosch. Tel: (021) 809 7380. www.oudelibertas.co.za

Durban
Botanic Gardens
Sometimes hosts outdoor concerts.
Tel: (031) 201 1303.
Sydenham Rd, Musgrave.

Johannesburg
Walter Sisulu National Botanical Gardens
Popular classical music in the gardens on summer afternoons.
Malcolm Rd, Poortview, Roodepoort. Tel: (011) 958 1750. www.sanbi.org. Open: 8am–5pm all year. Admission charge.

BARS AND PUBS
As is to be expected in a place like South Africa, there are a huge number of bars and pubs. Nearly all offer food and drink, but in a sports-mad country it's the establishments that screen sports matches that get really packed.

In these pubs and bars, most of the important international rugby, cricket and football matches are screened live, and the atmosphere in the better venues is second only to being at the game. The partisan fans welcome anyone who enjoys sport.

Golf, Formula One racing and English football are also regularly screened, as are special events such as the Olympics and the Tour de France. The more seriously sports-oriented pubs show the matches on big screens.

Cape Town
The Fireman's Arms
Fun 1906 vintage bar with a great atmosphere.
25 Mechau St, City Bowl.
Tel: (021) 419 1513.

The Sports Café
Screens endless international sport.
Upper Level, Victoria Wharf.
Tel: (021) 419 5558.

Durban
Billy the B.U.M.S.
A venue favoured by a generally young and affluent crowd.
504 Windermere Rd.
Tel: (031) 303 1988.

Johannesburg
Billy the B.U.M.S.
Owned by the same group as the Durban pub. Similar crowd, same sports.
Pineslopes Centre, Witkoppen Rd.
Tel: (011) 465 2621.

Pretoria
Billy the B.U.M.S.
Part of the same franchise as above. Most popular on Wednesday and Friday nights.
376 General Louis Botha Ave.
Tel: (021) 361 7049.

Sport and leisure

South Africans love sport, and many people spend their weekends either participating in games or watching matches live or on television. Football is by far the most popular sport, but cricket, rugby, golf and other games all have their fans. South Africa's good climate and varied geography also encourage watersports and adventure activities. Surfing, diving and sailing have large followings, and in recent years, adrenaline junkies have taken to skydiving, white-water rafting, shark diving and other exciting pastimes.

When *Bafana Bafana* ('The Boys'), South Africa's football team, lose a match, the event immediately sparks radio talk show discussions, letters to newspapers and heated debate in bars, on buses and on street corners. Fire the coach! Fire the administrators! South Africans don't like losing, and the response is similar if the national rugby team does badly or the cricket team fails to meet expectations.

Most sporting nations are passionate about their favourite team, but in South Africa, losses and victories take on a special edge because sport here often has a political sub-plot. For decades, black players were barred from participating in top teams, and sports administrators are still trying to ensure that equal opportunities are offered in terms of training, facilities and financial backing. Long denied international

South Africa has some great surfing spots

competition because of boycotts imposed in protest against apartheid, sports fans are eager for success, especially with the nation having hosted the Football World Cup, Rugby World Cup, Cricket World Cup, Africa Cup of Nations (football), the Africa Games (athletics) and several internationally important golf tournaments in the past decade.

South Africa has excellent sporting facilities, and the football, cricket, rugby and athletics stadiums compare with the best. Most provinces have world-class golf courses. A comprehensive list of all the sporting organisations in South Africa can be found on the website of **Sport and Recreation South Africa**.

Tel: (012) 304 5000. www.srsa.gov.za. The website includes contact numbers, scheduled meetings or matches, officials

Football supporters

and venues. It is particularly good for helping to plan which events to attend. Tickets for major sporting matches can often be purchased via www.computicket.com

Football

Football is by far South Africa's most popular sport. As is the case with football matches anywhere, attending a big match is a raucous affair and fans, some in fancy dress, whistle and blow *vuvuzelas* to urge on their team. Many teams have imaginative names, and the Dangerous Darkies (humorously named if politically incorrect) usually get thrashed by Kaizer Chiefs, the country's most popular team. Kaizer Chiefs have a fan club that stretches far into Africa, and a game against arch-rivals Orlando Pirates (both teams are based in Soweto) is one of the highlights of the season and heralds the same fan-frenzy as a World Cup Final.

South African Football Association

Tel: (011) 494 3522. www.safa.net

FOOTBALL WORLD CUP

South Africa hosted the FIFA World Cup™, the world's most popular sporting event, in 2010. Despite much scepticism in the Western press about South Africa's ability to organise and safely run the event, the tournament was a great sporting and PR success. It attracted around 400,000 football fans, many of whom would never have previously considered travelling anywhere in Africa, yet there wasn't a single major incident.

Although several of the newly built world-class stadiums are considered to be white elephants due to high maintenance costs, the tournament gave an incredible and invaluable boost to the country, both in terms of further uniting the populace and with many pleasantly surprised visitors planning return trips.

Johannesburg's showpiece FNB Stadium hosts football and rugby internationals

Rugby

Rugby fans are no less passionate, and the national team has a 100-year-old reputation for being one of the toughest and best in the world – a reputation that is sometimes hard to live up to in the demanding world of professional sport. Traditionally dominated by white Afrikaans-speakers, rugby is changing its profile to be more representative. One of its defining moments was Nelson Mandela holding the World Cup with the Springboks' victorious captain Francois Pienaar in 1995; this historic event, which transcended sport and brought together a violently divided nation for the first time, was the subject of the 2009 film *Invictus*.

South African Rugby Football Union
Tel: (021) 659 6700. www.sarugby.net

Cricket

Cricket is another sport at which South Africa has excelled, and one that is also changing its racial profile to become

GOLF

An increasing number of tourists are taking advantage of good weather and cheap rates to play on South Africa's championship-standard golf courses. Many exclusive housing estates have been constructed around courses designed by golfing legends Gary Player and Jack Nicklaus, among others.

The **Fancourt Country Estate** near George on the Garden Route, the **Gary Player Country Club** at Sun City and **The Pecanwood Estate** near Pretoria are among the best, but there are good courses in many other parts of the country. Most accept visitors.

Regional tourism authorities and hotels will have details of how to book a round, or visit: *www.golfinginsouthafrica.co.za*

more representative. The national team, the Proteas, did well in the 2011 World Cup, but not well enough to get further than the quarter finals.

Cricket South Africa

Tel: (011) 880 2810. www.cricket.co.za

Athletics

Athletics and boxing are also popular, and South Africans have performed well on the international stage. Many athletes compete on the professional athletic circuits in Europe and Asia. The country's long-distance runners are particularly successful, and a large number of marathons are organised every year.

Athletics South Africa

Tel: (011) 880 5800. www.athletics.org.za

Golf

South Africans have consistently been listed among the world's top golfers, although the sport has fairly limited appeal because of the cost of playing the game regularly.

South African Golf Association

Tel: (011) 476 1713. www.saga.co.za

The Fancourt golf course, near George, Garden Route

THE BIG EVENTS

Some of the most important events on South Africa's sporting calendar attract tens of thousands of participants and are among the biggest of their kind anywhere.

More than 14,000 athletes participate in the annual **Comrades Marathon** raced over 89km (55 miles) between Durban and Pietermaritzburg. Held on 16 June, it is regarded by many as one of the world's premier 'ultra-marathons'.

The **Cape Argus Pick n Pay Cycle Tour** is one of the largest bike races in the world. Every year in April, some 34,000 cyclists follow the spectacularly scenic 106km (66-mile) course that treats participants to stunning views of the mountains, sea and beaches.

The **Midmar Mile** in KwaZulu-Natal is another en masse sporting event in which thousands of swimmers race across the Midmar Dam.

Outdoor and adventure sports

As befits a country with lots of sunshine, outdoor pursuits and watersports are widespread. Many people waterski on inland lakes and reservoirs at weekends, much to the annoyance of those participating in the far more leisurely pastime of fishing. Away from the busy city centres, cycling and horse riding are popular activities.

Pedal Power Association

Tel: (021) 689 8420.
www.pedalpower.co.za

Gauteng Horse Society

Tel: (011) 702 1657. www.thsinfo.co.za

Motorsport South Africa

Tel: (011) 466 2440.
www.motorsport.co.za

Children

South Africa's good climate and open spaces make it a pleasant place for children to visit. In the cities, many teenagers hang out in shopping malls where they can go to see films, chat with their friends or get something to eat in safety. In many cases, the 'kids' culture' is very American, and Hollywood films, television, pop stars and even fast food often have an American orientation.

Travelling with small children

All the essentials from disposable nappies to DVDs are widely available. Bear in mind that if you are travelling, distances between locations can be very large, so carry books and games. Many South African parents resort to allowing their children to play

Playing in the sea at Camps Bay

endless mobile-phone games to ease the boredom.

There are excellent service stations on most major routes, and these have well-looked-after toilets, fast-food outlets and shops. Some even have small gardens where children can use up surplus energy.

Many South African fast-food outlets and family restaurants have children's menus on offer.

Swimming

Waves and currents along the South African coast can be powerful and unpredictable. Never allow children to swim unattended. Many more popular beaches have lifeguards, but the coastline is long, and it is not possible to patrol it all. Some beaches have tidal pools that make for safe swimming. Make sure that children reapply their sun block regularly.

National parks

All the national parks are well equipped to cater for children, and many rest camps have playgrounds and swimming pools. All the camps at the major parks are fenced and are quite safe. Do not let children, or anyone else, feed the monkeys or baboons.

In some of the larger parks, the hyenas have learnt that sometimes people throw supper scraps over the fence and make nightly patrols to see what food has been left out. Do not feed them and don't let children go up to the fence with food in their

Kleinmond Estuary, Western Cape

hands because hyenas have immensely powerful jaws.

Not all private game lodges allow entry to children under the age of 16 or, in some cases, 14.

Hotels

Some hotels can arrange a babysitting service. Both local and satellite TV services have a selection of children's programmes to choose from.

There are a wide range of entertainment parks, playgrounds and children-oriented activities available in most cities and towns. Many special activities and entertainments are organised over the Christmas and Easter holidays. Tourism authorities will be only too happy to tell you what has been arranged in their area.

Food and drink

South Africans are just as fond of local dishes as they are of Italian, Chinese, Indian and other cuisines from around the globe. South Africa is generally one of the world's more carnivorous countries, and there are very few dedicated eating places for vegetarians. That said, some restaurants will have at least one vegetarian option on the menu. Most people will find something that suits their preferred diet.

South African specialities

Meat features prominently in many meals, but although it is cheap by Western standards, it is still regarded as a luxury by poor people.

Biltong

Biltong is more than a snack food for many South Africans; it's almost a cult item. Connoisseurs will debate the fat content of the slices and the moisture content. It's the snack food equivalent of wine tasting.

Biltong, savoury dried meat, is sold all over South Africa. It is eaten pretty much any time that someone feels like a salty snack. It is usually made from beef or game animals, including kudu and eland.

Strips of raw meat are usually dipped in vinegar, coated in ground coriander seed, black pepper and salt and then hung in a cool dry place to cure. The early Dutch settlers originally used the recipe as a means of preserving meat.

Bobotie

Bobotie is ground lamb flavoured with turmeric, cinnamon and other spices covered with a form of custard and baked in the oven. It is usually served with yellow rice, raisins and stewed fruits.

Boerewors

This is a home-made farmers' sausage filled with a variety of meats and spices.

Bunny chow

Bunny chow is a Durban phenomenon. A half loaf of square-shaped bread is hollowed out and filled with curried meat or vegetables.

Koeksisters

Koeksisters are made from fried dough dipped in very sweet syrup.

Mealies

Mealies (corn on the cob) roasted over an open brazier are a popular snack food. They can often be bought on city street corners, particularly in Johannesburg, Soweto and surrounding areas. They are usually quite crisp and chewy.

Mopane worms

Mopane worms are an acquired, peppery taste, but worth a try. *Mopane* worms are the caterpillar of the emperor moth and are dried in the sun. They are very nutritious and are eaten as a snack or with *pap* (*see right*). They are often sold on the streets of Johannesburg, Pretoria and Polokwane and are sometimes served in restaurants that specialise in African food.

Pap en vleis

Pap en vleis (firm porridge and meat) is the favourite food of many South Africans. The meat is usually barbecued or grilled and the *pap* is a firm porridge made from de-husked maize and served with gravy.

Potjiekos

Potjiekos is meat and vegetables cooked in a heavy cast-iron three-legged pot. The pot (*potjie*) is placed over open coals and the stew is left to simmer for hours.

Prawns *peri-peri*

Prawns *peri-peri* is a recipe brought to South Africa by Portuguese visitors

Enjoy the local favourite *biltong* in a salad or on its own

from Mozambique. Prawns are coated in olive oil, lemon juice, garlic and *peri-peri* (hot ground chillies), and then grilled.

Sosaties

Sosaties (kebabs) are skewered lamb, beef or even vegetables.

Smoorsnoek

Smoorsnoek is a typical Cape Malay dish made with smoked snoek (a large predatory fish similar to a barracuda), chilli, onions, potatoes and sometimes tomato.

THE *BRAAI*

In simple terms, a *braai* is a barbecue where meat, poultry, fish or vegetables, or all of them, are grilled over an open fire.

The *braai* is a whole cultural experience that is popular among all sectors of the population. As with the *potjie*, everyone has their own idea as to the perfect recipe and method, but in the end the *braai* serves the same purpose for all – it's a great way to socialise, relax and enjoy good weather. Beer, wine and other drinks usually accompany the event.

WHERE TO EAT AND DRINK

Price guide:

£ = main course up to R80

££ = R80–100

£££ = over R100

Cape Town

Blues ££

Trendy seafood restaurant right over the road from Camps Bay Beach.
Victoria Rd, Camps Bay.
Tel: (021) 438 2040.
www.blues.co.za

Cape to Cuba ££

Friendly and fun, with a view of the harbour. Good seafood and old Havana décor.
Main Rd, Kalk Bay.
Tel: (021) 788 1566.
www.capetocuba.com

Jardine ££

Fantastic gourmet food and accompanying wines at reasonable prices in an old house in central Cape Town.
185 Bree St.
Tel: (021) 424 5640.
www.jardineonbree.co.za

Buitenverwachting £££

Old favourite on lovely wine farm. Great place to spend an afternoon or for dinner.
Klein Constantia Rd, Constantia.
Tel: (021) 794 3522.
www.buitenverwachting. co.za

Cape Colony £££

Top-class, refined restaurant with formal menu and excellent service.
Mount Nelson Hotel, Gardens.
Tel: (021) 483 1948.
www.mountnelson.co.za

Durban

Florida Road

A variety of cafés and bars on this busy street are good places for a cocktail or drink.
Florida Rd, Durban.

Royal Hotel £–£££

Several busy bars, serving excellent cocktails.
Smith St, opposite City Hall.
Tel: (031) 333 6000.
www.theroyal.co.za

The Havana Grill ££

Lively grill house serving excellent meat

and seafood dishes.
*Shop U2, Suncoast
Casino.
Tel: (031) 337 1305.*

Franschhoek
The Common Room ££
This café-style restaurant
offers lovely alfresco
dining, but is warm
inside in winter. Chic
venue with a top-class
reputation.

*16 Huguenot Rd,
Franschhoek.
Tel: (021) 876 2151.
www.lequartier.co.za/
cuisine*

Johannesburg
Kapitan's Café £
Wonderful curries and
atmosphere in a
restaurant once
frequented by Nelson
Mandela.

*11A Kort St.
Tel: (011) 834 8048.
Daytime only.*

Gramadoelas ££
The best-established
traditional South African
food restaurant in
Johannesburg. Also
serves dishes from
elsewhere.
*Market Theatre,
Newtown.*

Food and drink

Alfresco dining in Franschhoek, Western Cape

Tel: (011) 838 6960.
www.gramadoelas.co.za

The Grill House ££

Top-class steak, lamb and seafood. Try Katzy's next door for a late-night drink.
The Firs shopping centre, Rosebank (Corner Oxford Rd and Bierman Ave).
Tel: (011) 880 3945.

The Turtle Creek Winery ££

Great for a drink under the oak trees in summer and for sitting in front of an open fire in winter.
12 Wierda Valley Rd.
Tel: (011) 884 0466.

La Belle Terrasse £££

The restaurant of the upmarket Westcliff hotel has amazing views over Johannesburg's green suburbs and is perfect for drinks at sunset followed by an exceptional meal.
67 Jan Smuts Ave.
Tel: (011) 481 6000.
www.westcliff.co.za

Lucky Bean £££

Enjoy imaginative African and international food in the best restaurant of the relaxed, youthful and safe suburb of Melville.
16 7th St, Melville.
Tel: (011) 482 6424.

Knysna
The Oystercatcher ££

Oysters fresh from the sea and a great view of the lagoon.
Small Craft Harbour, Knysna.
Tel: (044) 382 6943.

Pretoria
Tings an' Times £

This popular reggae-themed nightspot also styles itself as a pitta bar, and has a variety of delicious versions of the humble flatbread on the menu.
1065 Arcadia St.
Tel: (012) 430 3176.
www.tings.co.za

Geet Indian Restaurant ££

Not for those with sensitive tastebuds, this restaurant offers Northern Indian-inspired cuisine.
541 Fehrsen St.
Tel: (012) 460 3199.
www.geetindian restaurant.com

Cynthia's Indigo Moon £££

Excellent meals in relaxed surroundings. Open for lunch and dinner during the week, dinner on Saturdays and lunch on Sundays.
283 Dey St.
Tel: (012) 346 8926.
www.cynthiasindigo moon.co.za

La Madeleine £££

Top-class Mediterranean-style restaurant, popular with politicians.
122 Priory Rd, Lynwood Ridge.
Tel: (012) 361 3667.

Stellenbosch
Die Mystic Boer £

For some authentic South African student culture, and the best pizzas in the Cape.
3 Victoria St.
Tel: (021) 886 8870.
www.diemysticboer.co.za

Spier Estate £££

Cape Malay buffet and other meals on a wine estate with lovely gardens. Café too.
Baden Powell Dr, near Stellenbosch.

Tel: (021) 809 1100.
www.spier.co.za

Wijnhuis Restaurant £££
Situated in a building
that dates back to the
late 1600s, Wijnhuis
offers an all-day Italian-
style menu and over
400 wines to choose
from.
*Dorpsmeent Centre,
corner of Church and
Andringa streets.
Tel: (021) 887 5844.
www.wijnhuis.co.za*

Tulbagh
**Paddagang Wine
House £**
Traditional Cape menu
includes smoked snoek
pâté.
*23 Church St, Tulbagh.
Tel: (023) 230 0242.*

Cape restaurateurs make the most of the wonderful scenery and great locations

Eating in South Africa

Whisky, cocktails or even beer – you can find your favourite tipple in most South African bars

Only a few dishes are truly indigenous to South Africa, and the country's culinary tradition is derived from the cuisine of a variety of countries. Many recipes have been adapted over the centuries with the inclusion of local ingredients and the introduction of innovative cooking methods.

Indigenous cuisine

Maize forms the staple diet of the vast majority of South Africans. It is usually prepared in the form of *pap*, a stiff porridge made from ground de-husked maize. It is served with meat or vegetables, but in poorer homes meat is something of a treat. *Pap* is also eaten with *maas* (milk curds).

Samp (whole de-husked maize) and kidney beans is another popular dish. Sorghum, a cereal indigenous to

Africa, sweet potatoes, onions, pumpkins and a variety of wild plants are also commonly used. Wild spinach is used to make a stew called *morogo*, which is often spiced with a chilli-based relish.

Many restaurants in the townships serve these meals regularly, and more and more upmarket restaurants specialising in African foods are creating stylised versions.

Other cuisines

Many South African dishes have their origins elsewhere in the world. Dutch, English, Indian and Malay people have all contributed to the style and flavour. The Malay slaves who worked in the kitchens of Dutch settlers helped introduce Indonesian sweet and sour dishes, pickles and chutney. The Indian population in KwaZulu-

Natal brought curries, samosas and naan bread with them, and some English-speaking South Africans still enjoy a Sunday lunch of roast beef complete with Yorkshire pudding.

Many of the dishes have been adapted over time and have become truly South African products.

Restaurants

South Africa has an enormous variety of restaurants offering international cuisine from around the globe. Italian, Indian, Portuguese, Greek, Chinese and Japanese food are widely available. French cuisine is also popular, particularly in restaurants based in the winelands.

Johannesburg has a growing Chinese population and, in the Bruma area, there are more Chinese restaurants than any other.

Meat forms the basis of many meals among those who can afford it.

Top South African chefs are highly skilled and produce world-class dishes

There are any number of grill houses that prepare excellent steaks, rack of lamb or pork spare ribs. Fresh seafood is usually available in restaurants along the coast and in Johannesburg, where restaurateurs have fresh fish, oysters, crayfish and prawns flown in regularly.

Several restaurants specialise in venison, and springbok, eland and kudu are often available, as well as game birds such as guinea fowl. Most restaurants cater for vegetarians, some with more skill than others. Of course, there are any number of fast-food outlets serving burgers, chicken or fish in forms familiar all over the world.

Drink

The country's favourite alcoholic drink is beer, most of which is drunk in the form of bottled lager, but traditional sorghum beer, or *mahewu*, is also hugely popular.

Wine is widely available, and many South Africans pride themselves on their knowledge of the local industry.

In KwaZulu-Natal, cane spirits are added to cola, and brandy is a favourite in Limpopo and the Western Cape. For the bold there are *mampoer* and *witblits*, which have a very high alcohol content and are made of just about anything, but usually grains or fruit. Treat with caution!

Accommodation

South Africa has a wide choice of places to stay, ranging from luxury resort and city hotels to backpackers' hostels, campsites, lodges on private game reserves and bed-and-breakfast guesthouses. Standards are generally high and good accommodation can be found even in smaller towns. Local tourist offices are happy to help visitors find accommodation of all kinds and to suit all budgets.

If you arrive at your destination without pre-booked accommodation, your best bet is to visit the local tourist office first.

Useful websites include the **South African Automobile Association** (*www.aatravel.co.za*) with links to all kinds of accommodation, and **Where To Stay** (*www.wheretostay.co.za*), which lists guesthouses, B&Bs and hotels with photos and full contact details.

Budget accommodation & camping

Backpackers' lodges with dorm rooms and basic doubles can be found in larger cities and along popular tourist trails. Guesthouses are a great budget alternative to hotels, and with rooms priced at around R400–700 can be very good value indeed. Most game reserves have campsites with shared ablution blocks and cooking facilities. There are also campsites at most popular beach and surfing resorts, with space for motor homes as well

as tents. Several companies hire out camper vans. Camping or staying in a camper van overnight is only advisable at secure campsites.

Hotels

Hotels are rated from one to five stars but the rating system is voluntary and some choose not to be rated. There are luxury hotels in all major cities and most resort areas, and there are also numerous smaller 'boutique hotels' in many cities and smaller towns.

National parks

Comfortable chalets with self-catering facilities are standard in most national parks and game reserves. Not all have en-suite facilities, but all are usually clean.

Private game lodges

Private game lodges – usually on the fringes of national parks such as Kruger – also offer luxury accommodation in the wild, along with guided game-drives.

Accommodation price guide

Accommodation prices vary widely according to season, so the price ratings given here should only be used as approximate guidelines. The pound signs in this section indicate the price of a double room per night and do not denote the hotel's official rating.

£ = up to R1,500
££ = R1,500–2,500
£££ = above R2,500

Johannesburg
Hilton Sandton £££
With 329 bedrooms, the Hilton combines the best of business and leisure facilities within secure landscaped grounds.
138 Rivonia Rd, Sandton.
Tel: (011) 322 1888.
www.hilton.com

Durban
Quarters Hotel £–££
A gorgeous, 24-room townhouse hotel made by converting four Victorian homes in Durban's trendiest suburb.
101 Florida Rd, Morningside, Durban.
Tel: (031) 303 5246.
www.quarters.co.za

Kruger National Park
Lukimbi Safari Lodge £££
Located on 15,000 hectares (37,100 acres) of unspoilt wilderness, this marvellous safari lodge offers 'Big Five' game viewing from open-top vehicles and is perfect for families, as it has child minders and a children's programme.
Kruger National Park.
Tel: (011) 431 1120.
www.lukimbi.com

Kwazulu-Natal
Pakamisa Private Game Reserve £££
Private lodge situated in a malaria-free game reserve. Offers eight spacious suites, a bar, restaurant and pool, as well as stunning views over the Pongola River Valley.
Tel: (034) 413 3559.
www.pakamisa.co.uk

Limpopo
Makweti Safari Lodge £££
In Limpopo's pristine, malaria-free Welgevonden Private Reserve, this superb lodge offers wilderness luxury.
Welgevonden Game Reserve.
Tel: (011) 837 6776.
www.makweti.com

Cape Town
Lagoon Beach Hotel £
Located on a huge stretch of sandy beach at Milnerton, a ten-minute taxi ride away from downtown Cape Town, the Lagoon Beach has an excellent restaurant, two pools, modernistic rooms and very helpful staff. This place is an excellent compromise between beach and city.
Lagoon Beach Rd, Milnerton.
Tel: (021) 528 2000.
www.lagoonbeach hotel.co.za

Boulders Beach Lodge ££
A cheap and cheerful, friendly guesthouse within hopping distance of the African penguin colony at Boulders. Comfortable cottage-style rooms, excellent

restaurant, great value for penguin lovers.
Boulders Beach Lodge, Boulders, Simon's Town. Tel: (021) 786 1758. www.bouldersbeachlodge. com

Cape Milner Hotel ££

Highly acclaimed city hotel in the trendy Tamboerskloof district, with chic atmosphere, boutique-hotel ambience and rooftop pool.
24 Milner Rd, Tamboerskloof. Tel: (021) 426 1101. www.capemilner.com

Cape Grace Hotel £££

This elegant hotel is the perfect base for first arrivals to Cape Town and is the best address on the lively V&A Waterfront. All 122 rooms have superb views of the harbour or Table Mountain (or both) and are full of personalised touches. Intimate atmosphere, stylish design and a great restaurant add to its appeal.
West Quay Rd, Victoria and Alfred Waterfront.

Tel: (021) 410 7100. www.capegrace.com

Winelands & Karoo
River Manor Country House and Spa £

It's worth visiting Stellenbosch just to stay in this gracious home from home, with 16 spacious and prettily furnished en-suite rooms in two historical Cape Dutch houses loaded with charm – as are the owners and their team. Two pools, pretty garden, the bars and restaurants of downtown Stellenbosch less than five minutes' walk away and an exclusive health and beauty spa as well.
The Avenue, Stellenbosch. Tel: (021) 887 9944. www.rivermanor.co.za

Mardouw ££

Superb family-owned, very professionally managed, country club-style hotel with extensive grounds. It has a golf course, pool, rose garden, and a range of extremely comfortable and charming rooms and suites.

Between Ashton and Swellendam on the R60, 26km (16 miles) from Swellendam, 20km (12 miles) from Ashton. Tel: (023) 616 2999. www.mardouw.com

Blaauwbosch Private Game Reserve £££

This luxury private game reserve with its extensive domain and game is the perfect way to experience the African wild on a visit from Cape Town. Very comfortable and spacious rooms, swimming pool, dining room and bar, plus dazzling starlit African skies and mountain views of the Eastern Cape.
Blaauwbosch, Karoo. Tel: (049) 835 9098. www.blaauwbosch.co.za

River Bend £££

Country house-style comfort in lovely suites with shared pool and excellent restaurant and bar on a private reserve adjoining the malaria-free Addo Elephant National Park.
Addo Elephant National Park.

Tel: (042) 233 8000.
www.riverbendlodge.co.za

Garden Route
Mitchell Street Village £

Tucked away on a quiet street five minutes from the centre of Hermanus, this is an impressive and friendly boutique guesthouse with unexpectedly upmarket facilities, including minibars in all rooms, two pools and pretty gardens. Highly recommended.
56–60 Mitchell St,
Hermanus.
Tel: (028) 312 4560.
www.56.co.za

Arniston Hotel ££

The best hotel on Arniston's seafront, with the colourful harbour and quaint old fishing village right next door. The exterior is plain, the rooms are bright, breezy and well appointed, and there is a pool, a gourmet restaurant and a more casual restaurant-bar. The ocean view is unbeatable.
126 Beach Rd,
Arniston, Bredasdorp.

Tel: (028) 445 9000.
www.arnistonhotel.com

Kurland £££

It is impossible to over-praise this absolutely idyllic manor house estate, with rooms set in thatched houses on a huge estate famed for its polo horses. An open-air pool is surrounded by wooded gardens, rooms are huge and bathrooms are sybaritic. Excellent breakfast and dinner. Fast Internet access.
The Crags,
Plettenberg Bay.
Tel: (044) 534 8082.
www.kurland.co.za

Pezula £££

Perched on a prime location on Knysna's Eastern Head, the Pezula Resort Hotel & Spa is South Africa's most luxurious resort hotel, with breathtaking views complemented by gourmet cuisine, lavish suites, a superb spa, championship golf course and vast range of outdoor activities. Friendly staff and outstanding personalised service.
Eastern Head, Knysna.
Tel: (044) 302 5332.
www.pezula.com

Rooms with a view of the pool at the Arniston Hotel

Practical guide

Arriving by air

South African Airways (SAA) has the largest number of services from the UK and Europe to Cape Town and Johannesburg, South Africa's main international airports. Flying time from the UK is approximately 13 hours.

Other airlines flying to Cape Town and Johannesburg from the UK include British Airways and Virgin Atlantic.

The main airports are:

O R Tambo International

This airport (25km/15 miles east of Johannesburg) serves both Johannesburg and Pretoria. The new Gautrain fast rail link (*www.gautrain.co.za*) connects the airport to Sandton station in Johannesburg's northern suburbs, and trains from there go to Rosebank, Johannesburg CBD and Pretoria. Taxis are also readily available and car rental companies are represented.

Help desk: tel: (011) 921 6262.
Flight information:
tel: (086) 727 7888.
www.airports.co.za

Cape Town International

A scheduled bus service connects the airport with the city centre (about 22km/14 miles away). Taxis are available and all major car hire companies are represented.

Help desk: tel: (021) 937 1257.
Flight information: tel: (086) 727 7888.
www.airports.co.za

Johannesburg International Airport is modern, and compares with the best anywhere

Lanseria International

Johannesburg's second airport is 40km (25 miles) northwest of the city, along the R512. It's increasingly used by budget airlines and is convenient for Pretoria and Sandton, although there are no public transport links here.

Tel: (011) 367 0300. info@lanseria.co.za. www.lanseria.co.za

Durban King Shaka International

Durban's brand-new airport lies 35km (22 miles) north of the city centre and serves several domestic and international destinations.

Help desk: tel: (032) 436 6000. Flight information: tel: (086) 727 7888. www.airports.co.za

Domestic airlines

SAA also operates to most neighbouring African countries and within South Africa, connecting Cape Town, Johannesburg, Durban, Port Elizabeth and Bloemfontein.

There has been a boom in low-fare airlines in South Africa in recent years, with half a dozen start-up airlines now connecting Cape Town, Johannesburg, Durban and other points. The main domestic carriers are:

Kulula

Internet bookings only. www.kulula.com

Mango

Tel: (0861) 162 646. www.flymango.com

SA Express Airlines.

Tel: (011) 978 9900. www.flysax.com

1Time

Tel: (011) 086 8000. www.1time.co.za

Velvet

Tel: (031) 582 8722. www.flyvelvetsky.com

International airline offices

South African Airways

Tel: (South Africa) (0861) 359 722, (international) (+2711) 978 5313. www.flysaa.com

British Airways

Tel: (011) 441 8600. www.ba.com

Virgin Atlantic

Tel: (011) 340 3400. www.virgin-atlantic.com

Arriving by land

South Africa has land borders with Namibia, Botswana, Mozambique, Swaziland and Lesotho. International bus services connect Johannesburg with all of these, but distances are long and roads (with the exception of Namibia) are poor beyond South Africa's borders. Anyone planning to travel onwards overland to Zimbabwe should check the current safety advice published by the British Foreign and Commonwealth Office or the US State Department.

Arriving by sea

The RMS *St Helena* sails several times a year from the UK to Cape Town, calling at Tenerife, the islands of St Helena and Ascension, and Walvis Bay in Namibia.

Sugarbush protea, Helderberg, Western Cape

Andrew Weir Shipping
Tel: (021) 425 1165.
www.rms-st-helena.com

Customs
Currency
Only R5,000 in South African Reserve Bank notes can be imported, while unlimited foreign currency and traveller's cheques are allowed, provided they are declared on arrival. Foreign passport holders may not take out more foreign currency than they declared on arrival.

Duty free allowance
400 cigarettes, 250g (9oz) of tobacco and 50 cigars, 1 litre (1³/₄ pints) of spirits, 2 litres (3¹/₂ pints) of wine, 50ml (1³/₄fl oz) of perfume and 250ml (9 fl oz) of eau de toilette. Also gifts, souvenirs and all other goods to the value of R500. No person under 18 is entitled to the alcohol or tobacco allowance. Duty is levied at 20 per cent thereafter.

Camping and caravanning
Both camping and caravanning are exceptionally good value (*see 'Hotels and Accommodation' on pp166–9*). The local tourist office will supply information about sites.

Children
See pp156–7.

Climate
See 'The land' on pp6–9.

Conversion tables
See p188.

Crime
See pp32–3.
Penalties for importing, possessing, using or dealing in illegal drugs – including some such as *dagga* (cannabis), which are widely available in South Africa – are severe.

Documents
Visitors must have a valid passport with at least two completely blank visa pages. Travellers with passports lacking blank pages will be refused entry. Visitors from the UK, Republic of

---

WEATHER CONVERSION CHART
25.4mm = 1 inch
°F = 1.8 × °C + 32

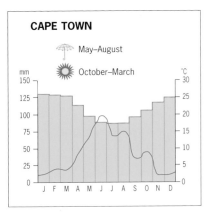

CAPE TOWN

May–August

October–March

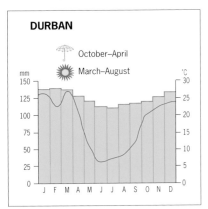

DURBAN

October–April

March–August

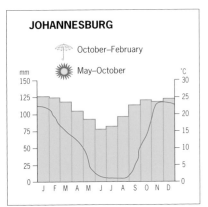

JOHANNESBURG

October–February

May–October

Ireland, EU, USA and Canada do not require visas. You may be required to show proof that you have access to sufficient funds to support yourself while in South Africa and you may also be asked to prove that you have a return ticket or the means to buy one.

Driving

Car rental

A valid national driving licence is required, as is an internationally recognised credit card. Cash is not accepted. Most companies will not rent to drivers under 21, while some specify 25 as the minimum age.

Because of South Africa's high crime rate, car rental companies in South Africa charge high insurance 'excess' levels (the amount you will have to pay if your rented car is stolen, broken into or otherwise damaged). You can reduce the excess by paying an extra premium and this is recommended, as is full collision-damage-waiver insurance. All rental companies offer unlimited mileage deals.

Avis

Central reservations: tel: (011) 923 3660.
Chauffeur drive: tel: (0861) 600 414.
www.avis.co.za

Budget

Tel: (0861) 016 622.
International calls:
tel: (011) 398 0123.
www.budget.co.za

Camperhire
Tel: (021) 683 0308.
www.camperhire.co.za

Europcar
Toll free in South Africa:
tel: (0861) 131 000.
International calls:
tel: (011) 479 4000.
www.europcar.co.za

Maui
Camper van rental.
Tel: (011) 396 1445.
www.maui.co.za

Tempest/Sixt
International calls:
tel: (011) 552 3900.
www.tempestcarhire.co.za

Thrifty
Toll free in South Africa:
tel: (0861) 00 211.
International calls:
tel: (011) 230 5201.
www.thrifty.co.za

On the road
The road network is excellent, and you drive on the left. The speed limit in built-up areas is 60kph (37mph), on secondary roads 100kph (62mph) and on freeways 120kph (74mph), unless otherwise indicated.

Traffic laws are strictly enforced: seat belts are compulsory; carry your driving licence; do not drive under the influence of alcohol.

Before your departure, check with the Automobile Association (AA) in your country whether you need an International Driving Permit to drive in South Africa.

Petrol stations are plentiful on major routes, infrequent on others. On major routes, most are open 24 hours a day and have excellent facilities, including fast-food restaurants and toilets. Most others are open 7am–7pm. Credit cards are not accepted at all filling stations: have cash as a back-up.

For expert advice, contact the

Automobile Association of South Africa
General enquiries:
tel: (0800) 84 322 (toll free).
Head office: AA House, 66 De Korte St,
Braamfontein 2001.
Tel: (011) 799 1001.
www.aa.co.za

Electricity
Power is delivered at 220/230 volts AC, 50Hz. Sockets accept round two-prong plugs. Adaptors are widely available in the cities and bigger towns.

Embassies and consulates
Australia
High Commission: 292 Orient St,
Arcadia, Pretoria. Tel: (012) 423 6000.
www.southafrica.embassy.gov.au

Canada
High Commission: 1103 Arcadia St,
Hatfield, Pretoria. Tel: (012) 422 3000.
www.canadainternational.gc.ca

UK

High Commission: 255 Hill St, Arcadia, Pretoria. Tel: (012) 421 7500. http://ukinsouthafrica.fco.gov.uk

USA

Embassy: 877 Pretorius St, Arcadia, Pretoria. Tel: (012) 431 4000. http://southafrica.usembassy.gov

Overseas

South African consulates in selected countries are listed below.

For further information, go to the website of the **South African Department of Foreign Affairs**. *Tel: (012) 351 1000. www.dfa.gov.za*

Australia

South African High Commission *Corner Rhodes Pl and State Circle, Yarralumla, Canberra, ACT 2600. Tel: (02) 62 727 300. www.sahc.org.au*

Canada

South African Consulate *15 Sussex Dr, Ottawa, Ontario, K1M 1M8. Tel: (613) 744 0330. www.southafrica-canada.ca*

Germany

South African Embassy *Tiergartenstr 18, 10785 Berlin. Tel: (30) 220 730. www.suedafrika.org*

United Kingdom

South African High Commission *South Africa House, Trafalgar Sq, London WC2N 5DP. Tel: (020) 7451 7299. www.southafricahouseuk.com*

United States of America

SA Embassy *3051 Massachusetts Ave, Washington DC 20008. Tel: (202) 232 4400. www.saembassy.org*

South Africa Department of Home Affairs

Subdirectorate: Visas. *Private Bag X114, South Africa. Tel: (0800) 601 190 (toll free). www.home-affairs.gov.za*

Emergencies

All emergency numbers – police, ambulance, fire and rescue services – can be reached on 112. For general emergencies from mobile phones, the number to dial is also 112.

Police
Tel: 112.

Ambulance, fire, mountain rescue, poisoning, air and sea rescue
Tel: 112.

Gay and lesbian

Gay Information and Travel Guide to South Africa
www.gaysouthafrica.net

Cape Town Pride
Website of the gay festival which takes place every February.
www.capetownpride.co.za

Club Travel
Travel agency.
Tel: (0860) 555 777.
www.clubtravel.co.za

The Gay and Lesbian Equality Project
Tel: (011) 487 3810.
www.equality.org.za

Getting around
By air
Several airlines operate domestic services between Johannesburg and major centres. They also fly to selected smaller centres. Several charter and safari operators fly to out-of-the-way places. Fixed-wing aircraft and helicopters can be chartered in all major centres.

By rail
There is an efficient long-distance service connecting major cities. Some routes involve overnight travel – services include sleeping berths, private compartments and a dining car. First- and second-class tickets must be booked at least 24 hours in advance. When booking, ask about discounts and special offers.

Overnight trains have dining cars for first- and second-class travel. Cabins are comfortably fitted out with seats that are converted to bunks at night.

Shosholoza Meyl runs comfortable passenger trains linking the main cities. Phone the central booking number in South Africa.
Tel: (0860) 008 888 (toll free).
International calls: tel: (087) 802 6674.
www.shosholoza-meyl.co.za

The Thomas Cook Overseas Timetable, published bi-monthly, gives details of many rail, bus and shipping services worldwide, and is a help when planning a rail journey to, from and around South Africa. Available in the UK from some stations, any branch of Thomas Cook, by phoning *01733 41677* or

South Africa's railways cross areas of wonderful scenery

through the website, *www.thomas cookpublishing.com*; in the USA from **SF Travel Publications** (*3959 Electric Rd, Suite 155, Roanoke, VA 24018. Tel: 1(800) 322 3834. sales@travelbookstore.com, http://travelbookstore.com*).

By bus and coach
A large number of daily coach services operate on intercity routes, day or night. Some services also run to Mozambique, Zimbabwe, Namibia and Botswana. Try to book your ticket at least 24 hours in advance.

Greyhound
Tel: (083) 915 9000.
www.greyhound.co.za

Intercape
Reservations and enquiries.
Tel: (021) 380 4400. www.intercape.co.za

Springbok-Atlas
Reservations and enquiries.
Tel: (011) 396 1053.
www.springbokatlas.co.za

Translux
One of the largest coach operators.
Central reservations:
tel: (0861) 589 282
or (011) 773 8056.
www.translux.co.za

The Baz Bus
Offers backpackers and budget travellers a service that takes in most of

A typical bus stop in rural South Africa

the major tourist attractions between Johannesburg, Durban and Cape Town, including the Garden Route. Flexible packages available.
Tel: (021) 422 5207.
www.bazbus.com

Hitch-hiking
Although hitch-hiking is widespread, as many South Africans do not own cars, it is inadvisable for tourists. Be cautious before giving lifts or accepting them.

Health
AIDS
As everywhere, be on your guard about HIV infection and take the usual

precautions. AIDS is highly prevalent in African countries, and South Africa is no exception (*see box on p13*).

Drinking water

Tap water is purified and is 100 per cent safe to drink.

Hospitals and doctors

Doctors are listed in local telephone directories under 'Medical Practitioners'. Most large hospitals have efficient casualty departments open 24 hours a day.

Inoculations

Visitors from most Western countries do not require inoculation certificates. It is best, however, to seek medical advice if travelling through other parts of Africa before visiting South Africa.

Insects – bites and stings

In South Africa, there are a number of insects or creatures that cause bites or stings. Most are relatively minor, but African bee stings can be quite virulent. Antihistamine cream is usually adequate to ease the pain, but medical advice may be necessary, especially if a child has an allergic reaction.

When visiting game reserves or rural areas it is a good idea to wear shoes at night, as scorpions are often out and about hunting. Some have extremely toxic venom and, should someone get stung, medical advice must be sought.

Blue-bottles, which sometimes wash up on beaches, are small floating creatures which can deliver a painful sting. Lifeguards usually offer assistance, but medical advice may be necessary.

Malaria and bilharzia precautions

Visitors to the Mpumalanga Lowveld, Limpopo, the Kruger National Park and the game reserves of KwaZulu-Natal should take anti-malaria medication as prescribed by a doctor.

It is inadvisable to swim in some rivers and lakes in the eastern and northern regions of the country, as the bilharzia parasite may be present.

Snakes

More than 130 species of snake occur in southern Africa, but only about 14 species are considered to be dangerous enough to cause death in humans. Most snakes move out of the way of people, and it is extremely unlikely that you will get bitten. (More South Africans die after being struck by lightning than from snake bites.) In the event of a snake bite, it is important to stay calm and get medical advice as soon as possible. Try to remember the colour and size of the snake.

Sunburn

Skin cancer is one of the most common cancers among South Africans. Try to avoid the hours when the sunlight is at its most intense – 11am–3pm – and remember that water provides little protection against ultraviolet (UV) radiation. Always wear a hat to protect against sunstroke. Sun protection measures are essential for young children. Use suncream with an SPF of at least 15.

For more information on skin cancer, and useful advice on protecting yourself when sunbathing, call the **Cancer Association of South Africa (CANSA)**. *Tel: (0800) 226 622.*

Insurance

Medical treatment must be paid for by the patient. It is essential to take out travel insurance which covers accidents, illness or hospitalisation, and that includes full emergency medical evacuation and repatriation. Travel insurance policies can be purchased through branches of Thomas Cook and most travel agents.

Drivers' insurance can be taken out through car rental companies. **SA Tourmed** sells travellers' medical insurance that covers the entire Southern Africa region. *Tel: (021) 979 4419. www.sa-tourmed.com*

Anti-gun sculpture on the Victoria and Alfred Waterfront

Language

South Africa has no fewer than 11 official languages, but most people manage to communicate through a combination of Zulu, English or Afrikaans. South Africans are multilingual, with many speaking about five languages. Most people in South African business and tourism communicate in English. Signage is also in English. Major newspapers are in English, Afrikaans and Zulu.

Place names

Throughout South Africa, many geographical names are in Afrikaans, Zulu, Sotho and other local languages. Many of the Afrikaans names make reference to animals or natural phenomena, such as snow or the colour of rocks. A lot of the names are an interesting, if rather sad, record of the former distribution of wild animals, many of which were hunted to the point of local extinction. Since the 1994 elections, the names of some landmarks that formerly had Afrikaans names have been replaced with ones from black languages. Pietersburg, originally named after a Voortrekker leader, is now called Polokwane after a local chief. Some Zulu place names are prefixed with kwa, which means 'place of', as in Kwambonambi ('place of the Bonambi clan'). Kwa is often used as a prefix to the names of rivers, mountains or plains.

Useful phrases

English	Afrikaans	Zulu	Xhosa
yes	ja	yebo	ewe
no	nee	cha	hayi
Thank you	Dankie	Ngiyabonga	Enkosi
How are you?	Hoe gaan dit?	Kunjani?	Kunjani?
Good morning	Goeie more	Sawubona	Molo
Good afternoon	Goeie middag	Sawubona	Molo
Good evening	Goeie naand	Sawubona	Molo
Goodbye	Totsiens	Hamba kahle	Hamba kahuhle
My name is …	My naam is	Igama lam ngu …	Igama lam ngu …
What is your name?	Wat is jou naam?	Igama lakho ngubani?	Ungubani igama lakho?

English	Afrikaans	Zulu	Xhosa
How much?	Hoeveel?	Yimalini?	Yimalini?
I am ill	Ek is siek	Ngiyafa	Ndiyagula
My child is sick	My kind is siek	Ingane yami iyafa	Umntwana wam uyagula
My car has broken down	My motorkar het gaan staan	Imoto yami yonakele	Imoto yam yaphukile
Show me the way to …	Kan u my die pad beduie na …	Ungangibonisa umgaco oya e …	Ungandikhombisa indlela eya e …
Where is a garage?	Waar is die naaste garage?	Likuphi igaraji elikufilphi?	Iphi igaraji ekufuphi apha?
Where is the post office/ bank/hotel?	Waar is die poskantoor/bank /hotel?	Iphi iposi/ibhange /ihhotele?	Iphi iposi/ibhanki /ihotele?
…the nearest hospital?	Waar is die naaste hospitaal?	Sikuphi isibbhedlela? esikufufphi?	Siphi isibhedlele esikufuphi apha?

Common terms

These terms are often heard mixed in with English in South Africa.

boss	baas	corn on the cob	mielie
pick-up truck	bakkie	bush medicine	muti
mountain	berg	South Africa	Mzansi
dried meat	biltong	only (on road signs)	net
farmer	boer	traffic light	robot
sausage	boerewors	herbal tea	rooibos
buddy	boet, bru, bra	witch doctor	sangoma
barrier	boom	illegal bar	shebeen
barbecue	braai	ugly, disgusting	siff
wild countryside	bundu	roundabout	sirkel
alcoholic drink	dop	kebab	sosatie
Johannesburg	Egoli	track	spoor
goodness me	eish	verandah	stoep
spring	fontein	a criminal	tsotsi
insect	gogga	kindness, compassion	ubuntu
party, fun	jol	countryside	veld
hill	koppie		
nice, great	lekker		

Internet

South Africa lags behind most of the developed world, and indeed behind many other developing countries, when it comes to public Internet access. Most upmarket hotels offer some form of Internet access (often at a hefty charge), but not all offer in-room wireless broadband and connections are often slow. In comparison with most tourist destinations worldwide, there are surprisingly few Internet cafés, even in major towns such as Cape Town and Johannesburg.

Maps

Excellent regional and city maps are available from South African Tourism and regional publicity associations nationwide. Most bookshops have a good range of local maps produced by Mapstudio. Jacana Media publishes some of the best maps and concise guides to the Kruger National Park.

Media

The South African Broadcasting Corporation runs more than 18 radio stations, broadcasting in 13 languages. It also broadcasts three major news and entertainment TV channels and one satellite channel. There are also a number of independent radio stations. Satellite TV offers a large choice of international news and entertainment stations and is widely available. Thousands of periodicals, journals, newspapers and magazines are published on a regular basis. There are a number of national daily and Sunday papers.

Money matters

Currency

The South African currency unit is the Rand, denoted by the symbol R (international symbol ZAR). It is divided into 100 cents (c).

Bank notes are issued in denominations of R200, R100, R50, R20 and R10. Coins come in 5c, 10c, 20c and 50c; R1, R2 and R5.

Exchange facilities

Banks may request identification when changing money. Shop around for cheap commission rates.

Money transfers

If you need to transfer money quickly, go to any of the major banks for assistance.

Credit cards

Most businesses, tour operators, airlines, hotels and restaurants accept international credit cards, including VISA, MasterCard, American Express and Diners Club.

Traveller's cheques and cash passports

Thomas Cook traveller's cheques free you from the hazards of carrying large amounts of cash and, in the event of loss or theft, can quickly be refunded. Cheques in either pounds sterling or US dollars are recommended. They can be exchanged in most banks, and in the major cities, many hotels, restaurants and shops will also accept them. However, a safe and easy-to-use alternative is a cash passport, a pin-protected pre-paid currency card, which you can load with South African Rand and use for purchases or cash withdrawals wherever the Visa Electron sign is displayed.

National holidays
1 January – New Year's Day
22 March – Human Rights Day
Variable – Good Friday
Variable – Easter Monday
27 April – Freedom Day
1 May – Workers' Day
16 June – Youth Day
9 August – National Women's Day
24 September – Heritage Day
16 December – Day of Reconciliation
25 December – Christmas Day
26 December – Day of Goodwill

Opening hours
Banks are open Mon–Fri 9am–3.30pm & Sat 8.30am–11am. ATMs are situated outside most banks and are open 24 hours a day.
Shops are usually open Mon–Fri 8am–5pm & Sat 8.30am–1pm. Some stores stay open all Sat & Sun.

Parks and reserves
National parks
These are run by the South African National Parks. Most parks in KwaZulu-Natal are run by Ezemvelo KZN Wildlife. The other

A sense of humour is essential in Africa

provinces also run the smaller parks in their areas.

Entrances to parks and reserves close at sunset, so aim to arrive well before that. It is best to do thorough research before booking accommodation to ensure that your wildlife experience meets your expectations. Travel agents will be willing to help or you can visit the following websites:
SA National Parks
www.sanparks.org
KZN Wildlife
www.kznwildlife.com
South Africa Tourism
www.southafrica.net.
Call Centre tel: (083) 123 2345.

Regional tourist offices will have details of smaller parks (*see regional tourism websites on p189*). Most travel agents

Pinelands police station, Cape Town

and the South African Tourism website have details of private game reserves and lodges.

Pharmacies

There are numerous pharmacies nationwide and they are easy to find. Should you require medicine after hours, it is best to ask at your hotel or B&B, as very few pharmacies stay open at night. Some private hospitals have pharmacies that are sometimes open later than others.

Places of worship

Churches of every denomination, synagogues, mosques and Hindu temples are all represented in abundance. Generally, South Africa's population is religiously oriented, and religious beliefs play an important role in public affairs.

Police

The South African Police Service (SAPS) can be contacted 24 hours a day (*see Emergencies p175*).

Many small hotels and B&Bs may also hire the services of private security companies that respond to burglar alarms. Management will give you details if applicable.

Post

Post office hours are Mon–Fri 8.30am–4.30pm, Sat 9am–noon. Letters and parcels can also be mailed via the **PostNet** chain of stores, which has branches nationwide (*www.postnet.co.za*).

Prices and tax

South African prices have increased considerably over the past few years so it is worth doing some research before booking accommodation and tours. Having said that, petrol is relatively inexpensive, as are local wines and spirits.

VAT, currently at the rate of 14 per cent, is levied on most items and services, including goods, transport, hotel accommodation and tours. You can claim VAT back on goods priced higher than R250 at the airport of departure, various harbours and customs offices. The original tax invoice, the VAT refund control sheet, your passport and the item are required. Please refer to the VAT shop at the international airport.

Public transport

Public transport in most South African cities is erratic. There are bus services in most of the bigger cities, but they tend to stick to limited routes, run infrequently and close down at night.

Minibus taxis are the most common form of public transport. The standard of driving, however, is usually poor, and the vehicles are often uncomfortable and sometimes unroadworthy.

Cape Town has a reasonable suburban and city rail service. Taxis can be arranged by hotels, restaurants or by looking in the Yellow Pages

One way to see Cape Town and other areas is by tour bus

Local musicians in the Cape Province

telephone directory. Ask for a quote before setting off.

Senior citizens

Facilities for senior citizens are not comprehensive. In general, expect discounts on cinema and theatre tickets and at some museums. If you feel you should be offered a pensioner's discount, it's best to ask.

The Association for Retired Persons and Pensioners
Tel: (021) 531 1768.
Age in Action
Tel: (021) 423 0204.
www.age-in-action.co.za

Smoking

As in many parts of the USA and Europe, there is a smoking ban in South

Africa. Smoking in public places is prohibited except in designated smoking areas and smoking establishments.

Student and youth travel
Hostelling International South Africa (HISA)
Helps provide student cards, information about discounts and other services.
1 Maynard Rd, Muizenberg.
Tel: (021) 788 2301.
www.hisa.org.za

Sustainable tourism
Thomas Cook is a strong advocate of ethical and fairly traded tourism and believes that the travel experience should be as good for the places visited as it is for the people who visit them. That's why we firmly support The Travel Foundation, a charity that develops solutions to help improve and protect holiday destinations, their environment, traditions and culture. To find out what you can do to make a positive difference to the places you travel to and the people who live there, please visit *www.makeholidaysgreener.org.uk*

Telephones
South African telephone call charges are expensive, and hotels add a significant charge to your call. Phonecards for public phones can be purchased in supermarkets, at post offices and so on. Other public telephones accept coins.

Mobile phones can be rented at airports and at mobile phone stores. Most UK mobile phones will work in South Africa. South Africa has an extensive mobile phone network, and renting a mobile phone is a far more reliable way of communicating than relying on public telephones.

Dialling codes
South Africa: *27*
Cape Town: *021*
Durban: *031*
Johannesburg: *011*
Pretoria: *012*

Useful numbers
Directory Enquiries: *1023*
International Operator (for booking or placing international calls): *0900*
International Directory Enquiries: *0903*

Time
South African Standard Time throughout the year is two hours ahead of Greenwich Mean Time (Universal Standard Time), one hour ahead of Central European Winter Time, seven hours ahead of US Eastern Standard Winter Time, and eight hours behind Australian Eastern Standard Time. South Africa does not observe daylight saving time.

Tipping
A 10 per cent service charge is generally expected in restaurants, not usually included with the bill. Raise the tip to 15 per cent if you have been particularly well treated.

Leave something for hotel staff, such as the chambermaids. Taxi drivers should receive 5 per cent of the fare on top, and luggage porters R5–R10 per bag.

Toilets

Most tourist venues, service stations and shopping centres are fairly well served by public lavatories. In nature reserves and national parks, standards of cleanliness are usually fairly high.

Tourist offices
South Africa
South African Tourism
Bojanala House, 90 Protea Rd, Chiselhurston, Sandton.
Tel: (011) 895 3000.
www.southafrica.net

Overseas
Australia
South African Tourism
Level 6, 285 Clarence St, Sydney, NSW 2000.
Tel: +61 2 9261 3424, fax: +61 2 9261 3414.
info@satour.com.au

France
South African Tourism
61 Rue La Boetie, 75008 Paris.
Tel: +33 1 456 10197, fax: +33 1 456 10196.
satour@afriquedusud-tourisme.fr

Germany
South African Tourism

Alemannia Haus, An der Hauptwache 11, 60313 Frankfurt am Main.
Tel: +49 69 929 1690, fax: +49 69 28 0950.
info@southafricantourism.de

Italy
South African Tourism
19 Via Mascheroni, 20145 Milan.
Tel: +39 02 4391 1150, fax: +39 02 4391 1158.
info@turismosudafricano.com

United Kingdom
South African Tourism
6 Alt Grove, London SW19 4DZ.
PO Box 49110, Wimbledon, London SW19 4XZ.
Tel: +44 (0) 20 8971 9364, fax: +44 (0) 20 8944 6705.
info@uk.southafrica.net

CONVERSION TABLE

FROM	TO	MULTIPLY BY
Inches	Centimetres	2.54
Feet	Metres	0.3048
Yards	Metres	0.9144
Miles	Kilometres	1.6090
Acres	Hectares	0.4047
Gallons	Litres	4.5460
Ounces	Grams	28.35
Pounds	Grams	453.6
Pounds	Kilograms	0.4536
Tons	Tonnes	1.0160

To convert back, for example, from centimetres to inches, divide by the number in the third column.

Practical guide

United States Of America
South African Tourism
500 5th Ave, 20th Floor,
Suite 2040,
New York, NY 10110.
Tel: +91 212 730 2929,
fax: +91 212 764 1980.
info.us@southafrica.net

Regional tourism offices
Cape Town Routes Unlimited
Tel: (021) 405 5000.
www.tourismcapetown.co.za
Eastern Cape Tourism
Tel: (0431) 701 9600.
www.ectourism.co.za
Free State Tourism
Tel: (051) 411 4300.
www.freestatetourism.org

Gauteng Tourism
Tel: (011) 639 1600.
www.gauteng.net
KwaZulu-Natal Tourism
Tel: (031) 366 7500.
www.kzn.org.za
Limpopo Tourism
Tel: (015) 290 7300.
www.golimpopo.com
Mpumalanga Tourism
Tel: (013) 759 5300.
www.mpumalanga.com
Northern Cape Tourism
Tel: (053) 832 2657.
www.northerncape.org.za
North West Tourism
Tel: (018) 397 1500.
www.tourismnorthwest.co.za

Travellers with disabilities
For comprehensive information – tours
accommodating wheelchairs, services,
handbooks and so on – travellers with
disabilities might find the following
organisations and websites helpful:
Accessible Cape Town
www.accessiblecapetown.com
National Council for People with
Physical Disabilities in South Africa
Tel: (011) 452 2774.
www.apd.org.za
South African National Council for
the Blind
Tel: (012) 346 1171.
www.sancb.org.za
South African Council for the Deaf
(DeafSA)
Tel: (082) 468 1032.
www.deafsa.co.za

Beware of the 'Big Five'

Index

A

accommodation 102, 103, 126, 157, 166–9, 172
African Art Centre 117
AIDS 13, 177–8
air travel 31, 170–71, 176
Alexandra 84
Amatola Mountains 74
amusement park 47
aquariums 49, 120
architecture 20–21, 64, 75
Arniston 58–9
astronomy 48, 81
athletics 155
Atlantic seaboard 50

B

ballet 146
Barberton 104
bars 151
battlefields 78, 132–5
Bayworld Complex 70
beaches 42, 50, 52, 53, 68–9, 119–20, 157
'Big Five' 108–9
birds 27, 58, 61
Bloemfontein 98
Blood River 135
Bontebok National Park 58
borders 79, 171
Bruma Fleamarket 88
buffalo 108
buses 177

C

cable car 49
camping 166, 172
Camps Bay 42
Cango Caves 62–3
Cape Agulhas 58
Cape Dutch style 20, 64, 75
Cape Flats townships 41–2
Cape Peninsula 50–53
Cape Town 39–49
car hire 32, 173–4
caravanning 172
cash passports 183
casinos 95
Castle of Good Hope 42
Cathedral Peak 128
caves 62–3, 105, 112
Cederberg Wilderness Area 59
Central Karoo 80–81
Ceres 59–60
Chameleon Village Lifestyle Junxion 94
Chapman's Peak 52
cheetahs 28
children 45, 47, 87, 103, 156–7
cinema 148–9
Clarens 98–9
Clifton Beach 42
climate 6, 30, 172–3

coaches 31, 177
Coedmore Castle 118–19
Company's Gardens 42–3
concessions 186, 187
Constitution Hill 87
consulates 175
conversion table 188
Cradle of Humankind 94
credit cards 34, 182
cricket 154–5
crime 32–3, 45, 172
Crocodile Ramble 95–6
Cullinan 96
culture 18–23 *see also individual terms*
customs regulations 172
cycling 155

D

dance 146
diamonds 76, 80, 82–3, 96
disabilities 31, 189
diving 120
documents 172–3
dolphins 55, 71, 120
dress 34
driving 31, 32, 107, 173–4
drugs 172
Dullstroom 104
Durban 116–22
Durban City Hall 119

E

East London 72
Eastern Cape 8, 70–75
Echo Caves 112
electricity 174
elephants 27, 33, 72, 108
embassies 174–5
emergencies 175
entertainment 146–51
Eshowe 136
etiquette 34

F

False Bay 52–3
festivals 22, 24–5, 71–2
fishing 104, 122
Fitzsimons Snake Park 120
food and drink 158–65 *see also individual terms*
football 152, 153
Fort, The 87
Franschhoek 60–61
Free State 8, 98–9

G

galleries 76, 143
   Ann Bryant Art 73
   Durban Art 119
   Irma Stern Museum 45
   Iziko-SA National 45
   J H Pierneef Museum 75

   Johannesburg Art 87
   Michaelis Collection 46
   Nelson Mandela Metropolitan Art Museum, The 70–71
   NSA 121
   Pretoria Art Museum 93
Garden Route 66–9
gardens 42–3, 45–6, 91, 105
Gately House 73
Gauteng 8, 84–97
gays 175–6
gemsboks 28
geography 4, 6, 8–9
George 66
Gingindlovu 136
giraffes 28–9
gold 84, 87, 104, 112
Gold Reef City 87
Golden Mile, The 119–20
golf 103, 154, 155
Graaff-Reinet 75
Grahamstown 71–2
Graskop 111
Greenmarket Square 43
Groot Constantia 43–4

H

hawkers 112
health 13, 31, 177–9, 184
hiking 69, 128, 129
Hindu temples 121
history 5, 10–13, 15–16, 78, 84, 86, 116, 132–5, 136–7
hitch-hiking 177
Hogsback 74
Houses of Parliament 44
Hout Bay 44–5, 50, 52
Hyde Park Corner Shopping Centre 88
hyenas 29

I

impala 29
insect stings 34, 178
insurance 173, 179
Internet 182
Isandhlwana 135

J

jewellery 141, 143
Johannesburg 4, 84–91
Juma Mosque 121

K

Kalahari Desert 79
Kimberley 76–8, 83
King William's Town 72–3
Kirstenbosch National Botanical Gardens 45–6
Knysna 66
Kommetjie 52
kudu 29
KwaZulu-Natal 8, 116–37

L

Ladysmith Siege 134
Langebaan 61
language 34, 180–81
leopards 108–9
Lesedi Cultural Village 96
Lesotho 138
lesbians 175–6
Limpopo 8, 114–15
lions 109
Lion's Head 47
Lipizzaners 89
literature 21–2
Long Street 46
Lowveld National Botanical Gardens 105

M

Magaliesberg mountains 96
Magersfontein 78
Magoebaskloof 114
map outlets 142, 182
marathons 155
markets 46, 87–8, 94, 121–2, 143–4
Matjiesfontein 81
media 182
Midlands Meander 130
minibus taxis 31, 32, 185
money 34, 172, 182–3
monkeys 33
mosques 41, 121
mosquitoes 34
mountain passes 64, 68, 81
Mpumalanga 9, 104–7, 110–13
museums 42, 58, 64, 76, 119, 134, 135, 137
   Amathole 72–3
   Apartheid 86–7
   Bayworld Complex 70
   Bo-Kaap 41
   Calgary Transport 73
   Campbell Collection, The 118
   District Six 43
   Ditsong Museum of Natural History 92–3
   Drostdy 64
   East London 73
   Freshford House 98
   Gold of Africa 43
   History 72
   Kimberley Mine 76
   Manor House Cultural 44
   Melrose House 93
   Museum Africa 88
   National 98
   National Women's Memorial and War 98
   Natural Science 119
   No 7 Castle Hill 71
   Reinet House 75

Robben Island Prison 47
Simon's Town 53
Slave Lodge 48
South African 48
South African Institute for Aquatic Biodiversity 72
South African National Museum of Military History 90
Voortrekker 131
see also galleries
music 19–20, 23, 149–51

N
Namaqualand 79–80
Natal Sharks Board 123
national holidays 183
National Women's Memorial 98
Ndebele art 114
Nelson Mandela Square 88
Nelspruit 105
Noon Gun 47
Noordhoek 52
North Coast 123, 126
North West 9, 102–3
Northern Cape 9, 76–83

O
opening hours 183
Orange River 6, 78–9
ostriches 62
Otter Trail 69
Oudtshoorn 62–3
Owl House 75

P
Paarl 63
packing tips 30
padlopers 27
Pan African Market 46
parks and reserves 33–4, 125, 139, 157, 166, 183–4
Addo Elephant National Park 72
Augrabies Falls National Park 78–9
Blyde River Canyon Nature Reserve 112
Bontebok National Park 58
Camdeboo National Park 75
Cape of Good Hope Nature Reserve 52
De Hoop Nature Reserve 58
Didima Camp 128
Giant's Castle 128–9
Golden Gate Highlands National Park 99
Greater St Lucia

Wetlands Park 124–5, 126
Hluhluwe Imfolozi Park 124, 125, 126
Ithala Game Reserve 126
Karoo National Park 81
Kenneth Stainbank Nature Reserve 118–19
Kgalagadi Transfrontier National Park 79
Kosi Bay 125
Kruger National Park 106–7
Madikwe Game Reserve 103
Mkuse Game Reserve 126–7
Mountain Zebra National Park 74
Ndumo Game Reserve 126–7
Oribi Gorge Nature Reserve 122
Pilanesberg National Park 102–3
Richtersveld National Park 80
Royal Natal 129
Suikerbosrand Nature Reserve 97
Table Mountain National Park 48
transfrontier parks 79
Tsitsikamma National Park 69
uKhahlamba Drakensberg Park 127–30
West Coast National Park 61
Wilderness National Park 66
passports 172
Paternoster 61
pharmacies 184
Pietermaritzburg 130–31
Pilgrim's Rest 112
places of worship 184
planetarium 48
Plettenberg Bay 68–9
Point, The 122
police 184
politics 11–13, 14–17, 44, 94
pony trekking 138
Port Alfred 72
Port Elizabeth 70–71
post 184
Pretoria 91–4
prices 167, 185
Prince Albert 81
public transport 31, 32, 100–101, 122–3, 176–7, 185–6
pubs 151

R
Ratanga Junction 47
Regina Mundi Church 91
rhinoceros 109, 125, 126
Rhodes Cottage 53
Robben Island 47
Robberg Peninsula 69
Rorke's Drift 135
Rosebank Mall Rooftop Market 87
rugby 154

S
Sabie 110–11
safety 32–3, 157, 171, 177, 178–9
San rock art 22, 128–9
Sandton 20, 84, 88–9
Sandton City 88
school holidays 30
scorpions 178
sea travel 171–2
senior citizens 186
Shakaland 123, 126
Shangana Cultural Village 105
sharks 123
shopping 43, 46, 87–9, 94, 112, 121–2, 140–45
Signal Hill 47
Simon's Town 52
smoking 186–7
snakes 70, 120, 178
South Coast 122–3
Soutpansberg 114–15
Soweto 84, 90–91
Spioenkop 134
sport 152–5 *see also individual terms*
springboks 29, 81
steenboks 29
Stellenbosch 63–4
street kids 45
student and youth travel 187
Sudwala Caves 105
Sun City 103
sun safety 178–9
sustainable tourism 187
Swartberg Pass 68, 81
Swaziland 139
Swellendam 64
swimming 157

T
Table Mountain 48–9
Talana 134–5
tax 141, 185
telephones 32, 187
theatre 22, 146–8
theme park 87
Thesen Island 66, 68
Thulamela 106
time differences 187
tipping 187–8
toilets 188

tourist information 34, 166, 188–9
townships 36–7, 41–2
trains 31, 100–101, 122–3, 176–7
traveller's cheques 182–3
Tulbagh 64
turtles 125
Two Oceans Aquarium 49
Tzaneen 114

U
Ulundi 137
uMgungundlovu 136
Union Buildings, The 21, 93–4
uShaka Marine World 120

V
Venda 21, 115
Victoria and Alfred Waterfront 49
Victoria Street Market 121–2
visas 172
Voortrekker Monument 94

W
Walter Sisulu National Botanical Gardens 91
Waterberg, The 115
Western Cape 9, 38–69
whales 54–5
White River 105
wild animal products 141
Wild Coast 73–4
wildlife 4, 26–9, 33–4, 108–9 *see also individual terms*
Wilson's Wharf 122
wine 43–4, 56–7, 58, 61, 63, 64, 141–2

X
Xhosa 21, 96–7

Z
zebras 74
Zulus 21, 96–7, 116, 123, 126, 132, 135, 136–7

Acknowledgements

Thomas Cook Publishing wishes to thank MIKE CADMAN and TREVOR SAMSON, to whom the copyright belongs, for the photographs in this book, except for the following images:

BIGSTOCK.COM page 37 (Craig Jewell)
DREAMSTIME.COM page 154 (Patrick Allen)
FLICKR pages 24 (tony4carr), 33 (Gerard) and 184 (Danie van der Merwe)
FOTOLIA page 124
ROBIN GAULDIE pages 21, 23, 72, 169 and 179
ISTOCKPHOTO.COM pages 67 (forgiss) and 159 (John Peacock)
JEROEN VAN MARLE pages 1, 25, 69, 86, 88, 143, 144 and 189
PICTURES COLOUR LIBRARY pages 89 (Clive Sawyer) and 147 (Roger De La Harpe)
SOUTH AFRICAN TOURISM pages 19, 26, 27, 28b, 32, 45, 46, 47, 48, 49, 50, 54, 65, 76, 78, 79, 82, 83, 96, 102, 103, 104, 107, 108, 109a, 109b, 121, 122, 123, 127, 128, 134, 136, 138, 139a, 139b, 150, 152, 153, 155 and 165
WIKIMEDIA COMMONS pages 28a (Winfried Bruenken), 29 (Thomas Schoch) and 177 (Andy Jou)
WORLD PICTURES/PHOTOSHOT pages 5, 176, 185 and 186

For CAMBRIDGE PUBLISHING MANAGEMENT LIMITED:
Project editor: Tom Lee
Typesetter: Julie Crane
Proofreaders: Penny Isaac & Caroline Hunt

SEND YOUR THOUGHTS TO
BOOKS@THOMASCOOK.COM

We're committed to providing the very best up-to-date information in our travel guides and constantly strive to make them as useful as they can be. You can help us to improve future editions by letting us have your feedback. If you've made a wonderful discovery on your travels that we don't already feature, if you'd like to inform us about recent changes to anything that we do include, or if you simply want to let us know your thoughts about this guidebook and how we can make it even better – we'd love to hear from you.

Send us ideas, discoveries and recommendations today and then look out for your valuable input in the next edition of this title.

Emails to the above address, or letters to the traveller guides Series Editor, Thomas Cook Publishing, PO Box 227, Coningsby Road, Peterborough PE3 8SB, UK.

Please don't forget to let us know which title your feedback refers to!